SPECTRUM®
Test Practice

With Free Online Resources for each U.S. State

REPRODUCIBLE

GRADE 1

W9-CCM-859

Published by Spectrum®
An imprint of Carson-Dellosa Publishing LLC
Greensboro, NC

Spectrum®
An imprint of Carson-Dellosa Publishing LLC
P.O. Box 35665
Greensboro, NC 27425 USA

04-286147784

The Common Core State Standards

What Are the Standards?

The Common Core State Standards have been adopted by most U.S. states. They were developed by a state-led initiative to make sure all students are prepared for success in college and in the global, twenty-first century workforce. They provide a clear understanding of what students are expected to learn in English language arts and mathematics.

These new learning standards for your child are:

- Rigorous.

- Based on the best available evidence and research.

- Aligned with college and work expectations.

- Benchmarked to the highest educational standards from around the world.

What Do the English Language Arts Standards Mean for My Student?

In grade 1, English language arts standards focus on reading, writing, speaking and listening, and language skills (grammar and usage).

These standards set expectations for what it means to be a skilled reader and writer in the twenty-first century. They provide strategies for reading fiction and nonfiction closely and attentively. They help students look for evidence and make critical judgments about the vast amount of print and digital information available.

What Do the Mathematics Standards Mean for My Student?

Examples of grade 1 mathematics standards include operations and algebraic thinking (adding and subtracting within 20) and number and operations in base ten (grouping in tens and ones).

These standards increase the depth and focus of math topics studied in each grade. Instead of sampling a wide variety of skills each year, students work to develop deep understanding and mastery of a few concepts.

Free Online State-Specific Test Practice

For additional **free** *Spectrum Test Practice* resources customized to your child's grade level and the U.S. state where you live, follow these instructions:

1. Go to:

   carsondellosa.com/spectrum

2. Click on *Spectrum Test Practice Free Online Materials* and register to download your free practice pages.

3. Download and print PDF pages customized for your state and your child's grade level.

Online Features Include:

- Links to Common Core State Standards information for your state

- A comprehensive practice test aligned to Common Core English language arts and mathematics standards for your child's grade level

- State-specific test items within the practice test, designated by this symbol: **1.**

  These items are aligned to the unique standards that have been adopted by your state in addition to Common Core State Standards.

- An answer key for practice test pages

How to Use This Book

Time spent practicing for standardized tests will benefit your child greatly. With the adoption of Common Core State Standards by most U.S. states, educators are relying more than ever on test results to compare your child's progress with that of others around the nation and the world. The resources in this book will help ease anxieties and prepare your child for test day.

What's Inside?

• **Lesson pages** contain sample questions and examples related to a specific skill. The assumption is that your student has received prior instruction on the topics. These pages can provide focused practice.

• **Sample tests** are shorter tests with questions about one subtopic.

• **Practice tests** are comprehensive tests with questions about the entire content area.

Practice Options

Choose how you will use the materials to meet the needs of your student.

• Select pages matching the skills your student needs to practice most.

• Assign lesson pages for practice throughout the week. End the week with a sample or practice test related to those skills.

• Administer a timed practice test in a quiet setting. For a first grade student, allow 1.25 minutes per question. After the test, check answers together and talk about what was most difficult.

Test-Taking  Clues

• Look for the symbol shown above throughout the book. Talk about the clues with your child.

• Read and review directions and examples. Talk about how test questions look and point out words and phrases that often appear in directions.

• Skip difficult questions, returning to them if time allows.

• Guess at questions you do not know.

• Answer all the questions.

• Try to stay relaxed and approach the test with confidence!

Name _____ Date_____

READING: WORD ANALYSIS

● **Lesson 1: Letter Recognition**

Directions: Look at the word your teacher reads. Mark the letter the word begins with. Example A is done for you. Practice with example B.

Examples

A. Which letter does the word **sand** begin with?

- (A) b
- (B) l
- ● s
- (D) c

B. Which letter does the word **large** begin with?

- (F) p
- (G) q
- (H) m
- ● l

Clue If you are not sure which answer is correct, take your best guess. Eliminate answer choices you know are wrong.

● **Practice**

1. Which letter does the word **park** begin with?

- (A) v
- (B) w
- (C) b
- ● p

2. Which letter does the word **dog** begin with?

- ● d
- (G) b
- (H) y
- (J) o

3. Which letter does the word **nice** begin with?

- (A) s
- ● n
- (C) u
- (D) k

4. Which letter does the word **talk** begin with?

- (F) j
- (G) f
- ● t
- (J) l

STOP

978-1-62057-593-2 *Spectrum Test Practice 1*

READING: WORD ANALYSIS

● **Lesson 2: Beginning Sounds**

Directions: Look at the picture. Listen to your teacher read the word. Listen to your teacher read the words to the right of the picture. Mark the word with the same beginning sound as the picture. Practice with example A.

Example

A. desk

A. chair
B. den
C. bat
D. man

Clue Say the name of the picture to yourself. Listen closely to the word choices.

● **Practice**

1. **rabbit**

A. man
B. bike
C. paper
D. ring

2. **mop**

F. miss
G. hill
H. clock
J. win

3. **bag**

A. vase
B. top
C. bell
D. fish

4. **tie**

F. tag
G. girl
H. shell
J. pin

STOP

Name _____ Date _____

READING: WORD ANALYSIS

● **Lesson 3: Ending Sounds**

Directions: Listen to your teacher read all the words. Mark the word with the same ending sound as the first word. Practice with examples A and B.

Examples

A. make
- (A) cat
- (B) rock
- (C) worm
- (D) pen

B. hive
- (F) web
- (G) fun
- (H) glove
- (J) tip

Clue Listen carefully to the ending sound of each word.

● **Practice**

1. star
- (A) mop
- (B) leaf
- (C) jar
- (D) five

2. leg
- (F) rug
- (G) gone
- (H) rich
- (J) grab

3. stew
- (A) net
- (B) wheel
- (C) barn
- (D) now

4. hit
- (F) dish
- (G) win
- (H) not
- (J) hear

5. bell
- (A) rest
- (B) hill
- (C) boat
- (D) cab

STOP

978-1-62057-593-2 *Spectrum Test Practice 1*

READING: WORD ANALYSIS

● Lesson 4: Rhyming Words

Directions: Listen to your teacher read the word. Choose the picture that rhymes with the word. Practice with example A.

Example

A. mop

(A)   (B)   (C)

Clue Look at the pictures. Say the words to yourself. Listen for the ending sound.

● Practice

1. **dog**

(A)   (B)   (C)

2. **hat**

(F)   (G)   (H)

3. **rock**

(A)   (B)   (C)

STOP

READING: WORD ANALYSIS

● **Lesson 5: Word Recognition**

Directions: Listen to your teacher read the word. Notice the underlined part. Then listen as your teacher reads the word choices. Listen for the word with the same sound as the underlined part and mark it. Practice with examples A and B.

Examples

A. mud
- Ⓐ but
- Ⓑ sock
- Ⓒ shell
- Ⓓ cat

B. pound
- Ⓕ snow
- Ⓖ spent
- Ⓗ loud
- Ⓙ rider

Clue Do numbers 1–4 the same way. You may ask your teacher to repeat an item after all of the problems have been read one time.

● **Practice**

1. **rose**
- Ⓐ rule
- Ⓑ bake
- Ⓒ pony
- Ⓓ nine

2. **spoon**
- Ⓕ here
- Ⓖ smooth
- Ⓗ after
- Ⓙ chip

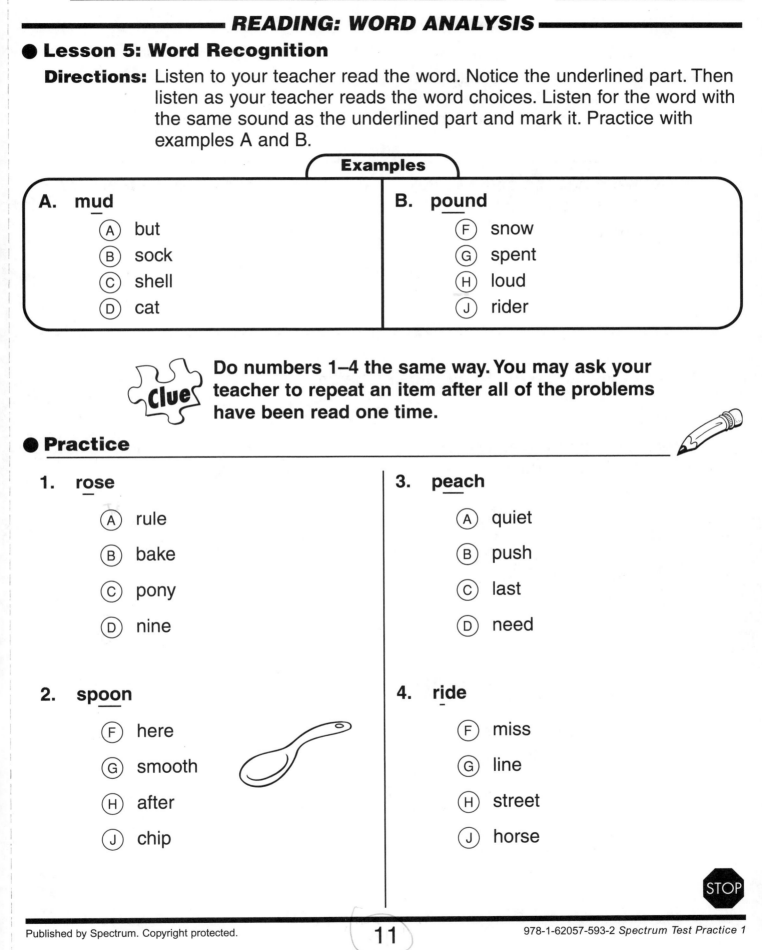

3. **peach**
- Ⓐ quiet
- Ⓑ push
- Ⓒ last
- Ⓓ need

4. **ride**
- Ⓕ miss
- Ⓖ line
- Ⓗ street
- Ⓙ horse

STOP

Name _____   Date _____

READING: WORD ANALYSIS

● **Lesson 6: Vowel Sounds and Sight Words**

Directions: Listen as your teacher reads the question and says the name of the picture. Then listen as your teacher reads the word choices. Choose the best answer. Example A is done for you. Practice with example B.

Examples

A. **What word has the same vowel sound as the picture?**

- Ⓐ pen
- Ⓑ spoon
- Ⓒ kite
- Ⓓ chip

B. **What word rhymes with shell?**

- Ⓕ smell
- Ⓖ dog
- Ⓗ rode
- Ⓙ mile

Clue Listen to all choices before you mark your answer.

● **Practice**

1. **What word has the same vowel sound as the picture?**

- Ⓐ mouse
- Ⓑ long
- Ⓒ tick
- Ⓓ spoon

2. **What word has the same vowel sound as the picture?**

- Ⓕ bead
- Ⓖ hive
- Ⓗ quilt
- Ⓙ apple

3. **What word has the same vowel sound as might?**

- Ⓐ pin
- Ⓑ time
- Ⓒ from
- Ⓓ soul

4. **What word rhymes with tough?**

- Ⓕ crow
- Ⓖ pool
- Ⓗ puff
- Ⓙ ton

STOP

978-1-62057-593-2 *Spectrum Test Practice 1*

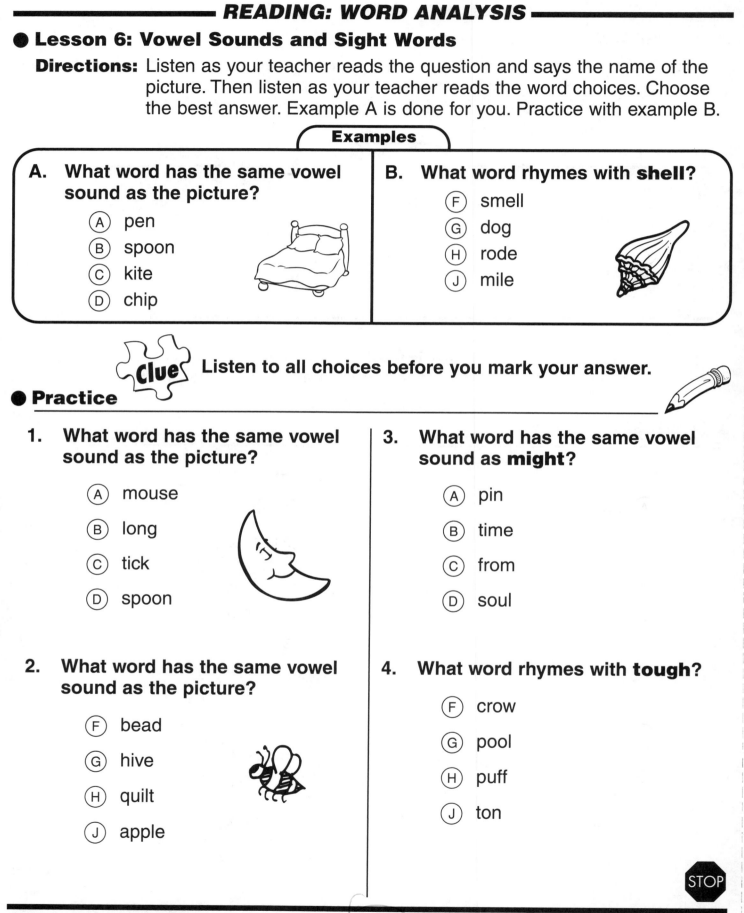

READING: WORD ANALYSIS

● Lesson 7: Word Study

Directions: Listen as your teacher reads the word choices. Mark the word that is a compound word. Practice with example A.

Directions: Listen as your teacher reads the sentence and the word choices. One will fill in the blank. Mark your choice. Practice with example B.

Examples

A.
- (A) airplane
- (B) ringer
- (C) tune

B. The dog _____ its food.
- (F) eat
- (G) ate
- (H) eating

Clue Listen carefully each time your teacher reads directions. The directions may change.

● Practice

1.
- (A) toolbox
- (B) kitchen
- (C) gate

2.
- (F) warning
- (G) flowerpot
- (H) glasses

3.
- (A) teacup
- (B) pencil
- (C) jumping

4. I am _____ than you.
- (F) big
- (G) bigger
- (H) biggest

5. I _____ books.
- (A) readed
- (B) reads
- (C) read

6. He _____ hot.
- (F) weren't
- (G) wasn't
- (H) won't

STOP

Name _____ Date _____

READING: WORD ANALYSIS
SAMPLE TEST

Directions: Listen as your teacher reads the problems and answer choices. Mark the best answer. Practice with example A.

Example

A. **What picture starts with the same sound as nut?**

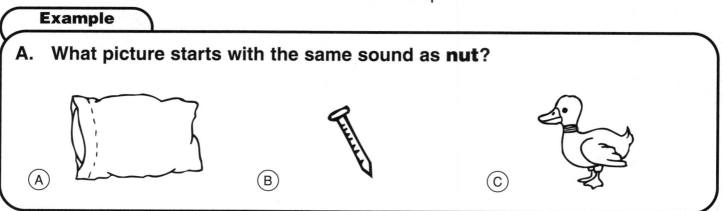

Ⓐ   Ⓑ   Ⓒ

1. **What picture begins with the same sound as cat?**

Ⓐ   Ⓑ   Ⓒ

2. **What word begins with the same sound as the picture?**

   Ⓕ   bat
   Ⓖ   pig
   Ⓗ   kite
   Ⓙ   sun

3. **What letters show the beginning sound of the picture?**

   Ⓐ   gl
   Ⓑ   tr
   Ⓒ   gr
   Ⓓ   sl

4. **What word ends with the same sound as get?**

   Ⓕ   tip
   Ⓖ   sat
   Ⓗ   run
   Ⓙ   girl

5. **What word ends with the same sound as rash?**

   Ⓐ   with
   Ⓑ   luck
   Ⓒ   push
   Ⓓ   itch

GO ON

Name _____   Date_____

Directions: Listen as your teacher reads the words and answer choices. Look at the underlined part. Which word has the same sound as the underlined part? Practice with examples B and C.

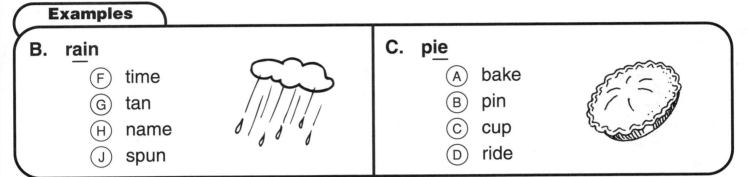

Examples

B. r<u>ai</u>n
- Ⓕ time
- Ⓖ tan
- Ⓗ name
- Ⓙ spun

C. p<u>ie</u>
- Ⓐ bake
- Ⓑ pin
- Ⓒ cup
- Ⓓ ride

6. p<u>i</u>n
- Ⓕ tip
- Ⓖ had
- Ⓗ shut
- Ⓙ peel

7. m<u>ai</u>l
- Ⓐ cat
- Ⓑ trade
- Ⓒ kit
- Ⓓ push

8. s<u>a</u>t
- Ⓕ miss
- Ⓖ pit
- Ⓗ ban
- Ⓙ same

9. sp<u>oo</u>n
- Ⓐ touch
- Ⓑ pool
- Ⓒ tot
- Ⓓ pad

10. m<u>ee</u>t
- Ⓕ tick
- Ⓖ piece
- Ⓗ bun
- Ⓙ stem

11. h<u>au</u>nt
- Ⓐ paw
- Ⓑ hat
- Ⓒ hunt
- Ⓓ stir

GO ON

READING: WORD ANALYSIS
SAMPLE TEST (cont.)

Directions: Listen as your teacher reads the words. Take away the first letter sound. Replace it with another sound. Mark the picture of the new word it makes.

12. bun

F   G   H

13. tail

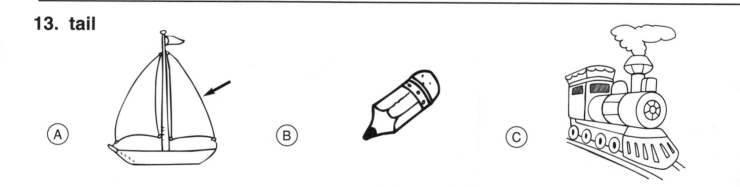

A   B   C

● **Directions:** Choose the beginning sound that will make the word shown next to the picture.

14. ___ill

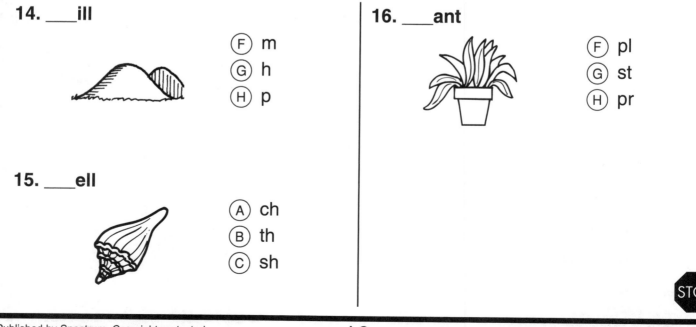

F m
G h
H p

16. ___ant

F pl
G st
H pr

15. ___ell

A ch
B th
C sh

STOP

READING: VOCABULARY

● **Lesson 8: Picture Vocabulary**

Directions: Listen to your teacher read the sentence. Choose the picture that finishes the sentence. Practice with example A.

Example

A.   **Bill drinks _____ .**

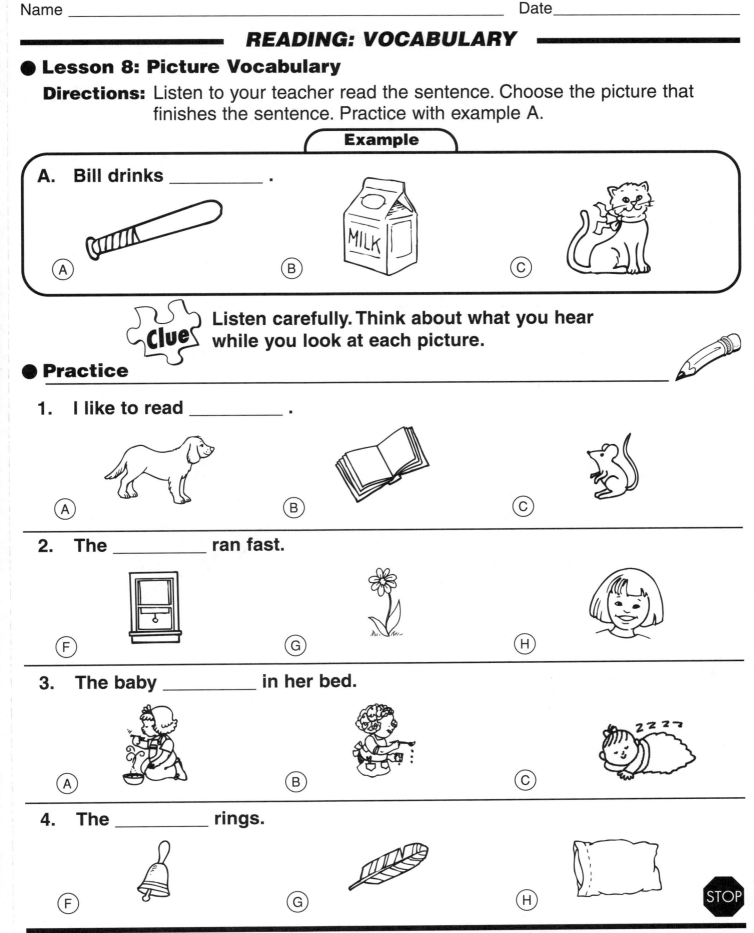

Ⓐ   Ⓑ   Ⓒ

Clue   Listen carefully. Think about what you hear while you look at each picture.

● **Practice**

1.   **I like to read _____ .**

Ⓐ   Ⓑ   Ⓒ

2.   **The _____ ran fast.**

Ⓕ   Ⓖ   Ⓗ

3.   **The baby _____ in her bed.**

Ⓐ   Ⓑ   Ⓒ

4.   **The _____ rings.**

Ⓕ   Ⓖ   Ⓗ

STOP

READING: VOCABULARY

● **Lesson 9: Word Reading**

Directions: Look at the picture. Listen as your teacher reads the word choices. Mark the word that matches the picture. Practice with examples A and B.

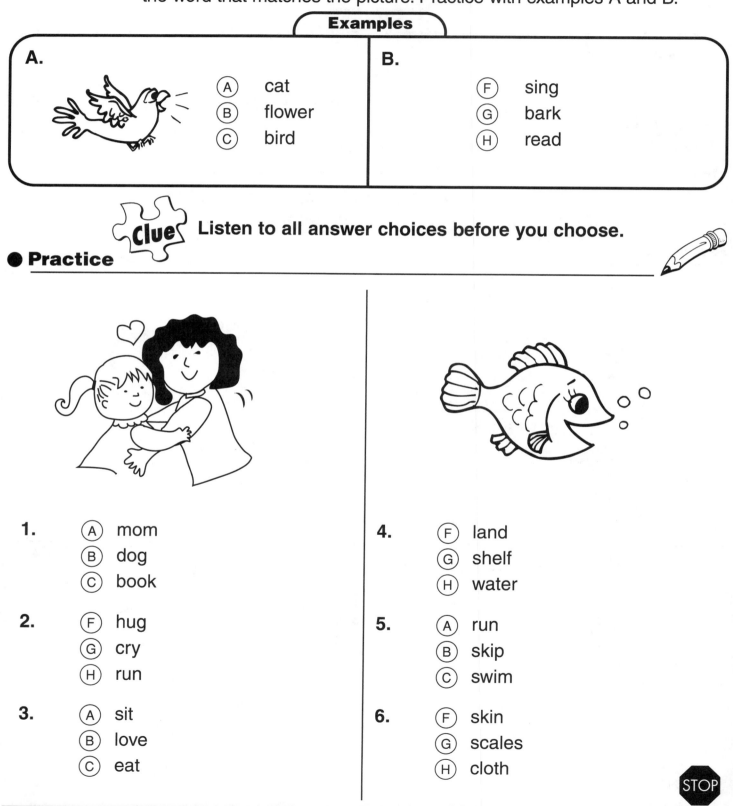

Examples

A.
- (A) cat
- (B) flower
- (C) bird

B.
- (F) sing
- (G) bark
- (H) read

Clue Listen to all answer choices before you choose.

● **Practice**

1.
- (A) mom
- (B) dog
- (C) book

2.
- (F) hug
- (G) cry
- (H) run

3.
- (A) sit
- (B) love
- (C) eat

4.
- (F) land
- (G) shelf
- (H) water

5.
- (A) run
- (B) skip
- (C) swim

6.
- (F) skin
- (G) scales
- (H) cloth

STOP

READING: VOCABULARY

● Lesson 10: Word Meaning

Directions: Listen to your teacher read each phrase and the word choices. Mark the word that matches the phrase. Practice with examples A and B.

Examples

A. **to move fast...**
- Ⓐ crawl
- Ⓑ run
- Ⓒ walk
- Ⓓ sit

B. **a cold thing...**
- Ⓕ ice
- Ⓖ fire
- Ⓗ sun
- Ⓙ stove

Clue Be sure about your answer.

● Practice

1. **a thing that flies...**
- Ⓐ pen
- Ⓑ book
- Ⓒ bird
- Ⓓ cup

2. **a thing that sings...**
- Ⓕ chair
- Ⓖ girl
- Ⓗ nest
- Ⓙ paper

3. **to drink a little...**
- Ⓐ spill
- Ⓑ tip
- Ⓒ sip
- Ⓓ toss

4. **to stay on top of water...**
- Ⓕ float
- Ⓖ sink
- Ⓗ pin
- Ⓙ zip

5. **noise a dog makes...**
- Ⓐ bark
- Ⓑ purr
- Ⓒ cut
- Ⓓ land

6. **a food...**
- Ⓕ wood
- Ⓖ cart
- Ⓗ apple
- Ⓙ bed

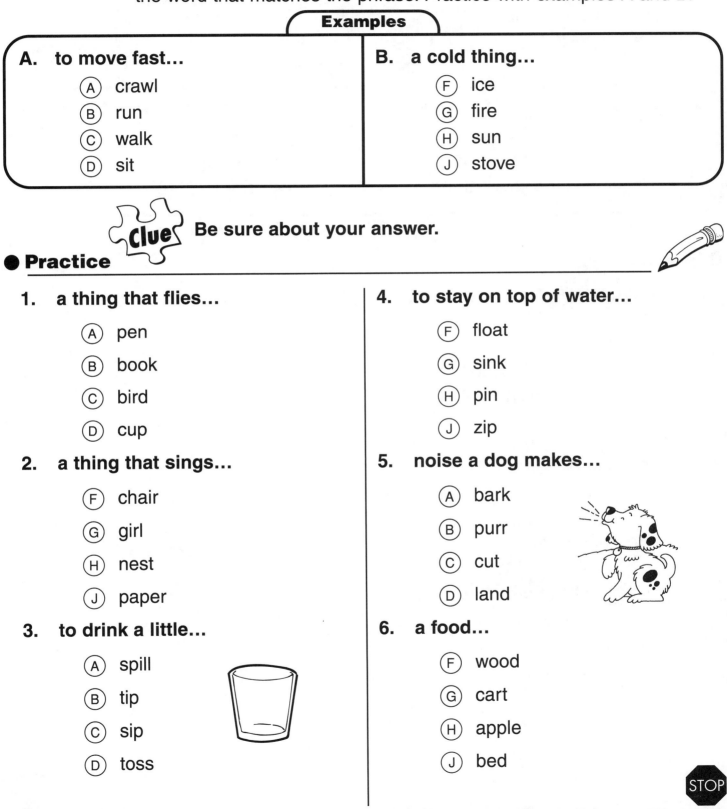

STOP

READING: VOCABULARY

● **Lesson 11: Word Parts**

Directions: For numbers 1–3, choose the phrase that has the same meaning as the underlined word. Practice with example A.

Directions: For numbers 4–6, choose the word that has the same root as the underlined word. Practice with example B.

Examples

A. **Please help me <u>untie</u> the knot.**
- Ⓐ tie the knot again
- Ⓑ take the knot apart
- Ⓒ make the knot tighter

B. **I can teach you how to <u>tell</u> time.**
- Ⓕ telling
- Ⓖ saying
- Ⓗ say

● **Practice**

1. **You look <u>hopeful</u> that you will win.**
- Ⓐ full of hope
- Ⓑ without any hope
- Ⓒ hoping again

2. **We had to <u>return</u> because we forgot our <u>lunch</u>.**
- Ⓕ turn over
- Ⓖ turn forward
- Ⓗ turn back

3. **We <u>distrust</u> the growling dog.**
- Ⓐ don't trust
- Ⓑ really trust
- Ⓒ trust again

4. **We had a <u>laugh</u> at the joke.**
- Ⓕ laughing
- Ⓖ funny
- Ⓗ happy

5. **That story made me <u>cry</u>.**
- Ⓐ laugh
- Ⓑ cried
- Ⓒ sad

6. **How fast can you <u>run</u>?**
- Ⓕ walk
- Ⓖ running
- Ⓗ skip

STOP

Name _____   Date _____

READING: VOCABULARY

● **Lesson 12: Word Relationships**

Directions: Listen to your teacher read each word. Choose the group that fits all the words. Practice with examples A and B.

Examples

A. robin, crow, dove
   - Ⓐ dogs
   - Ⓑ birds
   - Ⓒ trees

B. milk, juice, water
   - Ⓕ things you drink
   - Ⓖ things you wear
   - Ⓗ things you ride

● **Practice**

1. **basketball, football, soccer, baseball**
   - Ⓐ clothes
   - Ⓑ mittens
   - Ⓒ sports

2. **apple, pear, orange, lemon**
   - Ⓕ colors
   - Ⓖ pets
   - Ⓗ fruit

3. **horse, goat, cow, dog**
   - Ⓐ animals with four legs
   - Ⓑ animals that fly
   - Ⓒ animals that bark

4. **car, truck, wagon, bike**
   - Ⓕ things with wheels
   - Ⓖ things with engines
   - Ⓗ things with two wheels

5. **coat, jacket, sweater, scarf**
   - Ⓐ clothes for hot weather
   - Ⓑ clothes for rainy weather
   - Ⓒ clothes for cold weather

6. **tiny, mini, wee, little**
   - Ⓕ words for something quiet
   - Ⓖ words for something big
   - Ⓗ words for something small

STOP

READING: VOCABULARY

● **Lesson 13: Synonyms**

Directions: Listen to your teacher read the sentence and word choices. Look at the underlined part. Mark the word that means about the same. Practice with examples A and B.

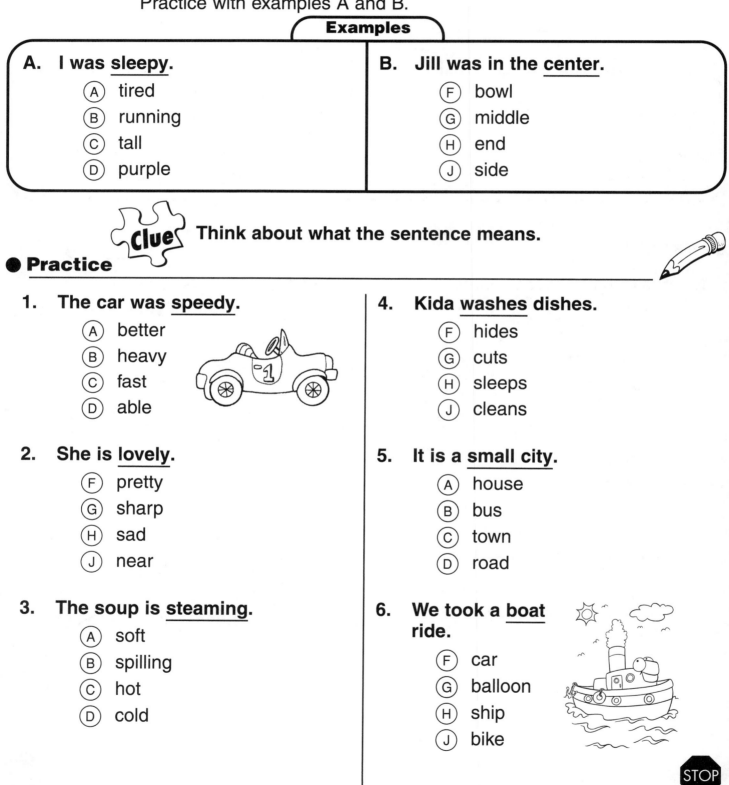

Examples

A.   I was <u>sleepy</u>.

Ⓐ tired
Ⓑ running
Ⓒ tall
Ⓓ purple

B.   Jill was in the <u>center</u>.

Ⓕ bowl
Ⓖ middle
Ⓗ end
Ⓙ side

Clue Think about what the sentence means.

● **Practice**

1.   **The car was <u>speedy</u>.**

Ⓐ better
Ⓑ heavy
Ⓒ fast
Ⓓ able

2.   **She is <u>lovely</u>.**

Ⓕ pretty
Ⓖ sharp
Ⓗ sad
Ⓙ near

3.   **The soup is <u>steaming</u>.**

Ⓐ soft
Ⓑ spilling
Ⓒ hot
Ⓓ cold

4.   **Kida <u>washes</u> dishes.**

Ⓕ hides
Ⓖ cuts
Ⓗ sleeps
Ⓙ cleans

5.   **It is a <u>small city</u>.**

Ⓐ house
Ⓑ bus
Ⓒ town
Ⓓ road

6.   **We took a <u>boat</u> ride.**

Ⓕ car
Ⓖ balloon
Ⓗ ship
Ⓙ bike

STOP

READING: VOCABULARY

● **Lesson 14: Antonyms**

Directions: Listen to your teacher read the sentence and word choices. Look at the underlined part. Mark the word that means the opposite. Practice with examples A and B.

Examples

A. **This is wet.**
- Ⓐ big
- Ⓑ brown
- Ⓒ dry
- Ⓓ soaked

B. **The rock is heavy.**
- Ⓕ cold
- Ⓖ hard
- Ⓗ dirty
- Ⓙ light

 Clue Remember, the correct answer is the opposite of the underlined part.

● **Practice**

1. **The bear is tame.**
- Ⓐ black
- Ⓑ wild
- Ⓒ hungry
- Ⓓ big

2. **Susie whispered the secret.**
- Ⓕ yelled
- Ⓖ tapped
- Ⓗ cried
- Ⓙ wrote

3. **Why is it so little?**
- Ⓐ loud
- Ⓑ bad
- Ⓒ big
- Ⓓ short

4. **I run very fast.**
- Ⓕ slow
- Ⓖ quick
- Ⓗ around
- Ⓙ loud

5. **This is easy.**
- Ⓐ less
- Ⓑ home
- Ⓒ simple
- Ⓓ hard

6. **Jordan was sick.**
- Ⓕ ill
- Ⓖ happy
- Ⓗ well
- Ⓙ tiny

STOP

READING: VOCABULARY

● **Lesson 15: Words in Context**

Directions: Listen to your teacher read the sentence and word choices. Choose the word that completes the sentence. Practice with examples A and B.

Examples

A. The _____ was green. It hopped far.
- (A) dog
- (B) rabbit
- (C) frog
- (D) boy

B. The _____ was long. It had 13 cars.
- (F) string
- (G) train
- (H) paper
- (J) hair

Clue When you think you hear the correct answer, put your finger next to it. Listen to all of the choices.

● **Practice**

1. Sam sat on the _____ . He soon fell asleep.
- (A) ice
- (B) chair
- (C) hammer
- (D) nail

3. There are four _____ on the shelf. Tuti read them all.
- (A) cats
- (B) animals
- (C) suns
- (D) books

2. The bee flew to its _____ . It went inside.
- (F) corner
- (G) cup
- (H) hive
- (J) honey

4. The joke was _____ . We all smiled.
- (F) funny
- (G) sad
- (H) blue
- (J) bread

STOP

Name _____ Date_____

READING: VOCABULARY
SAMPLE TEST

Directions: Listen to your teacher read the phrase. Choose the picture that shows what the words mean. Practice with example A.

Example

A. **A red fruit**

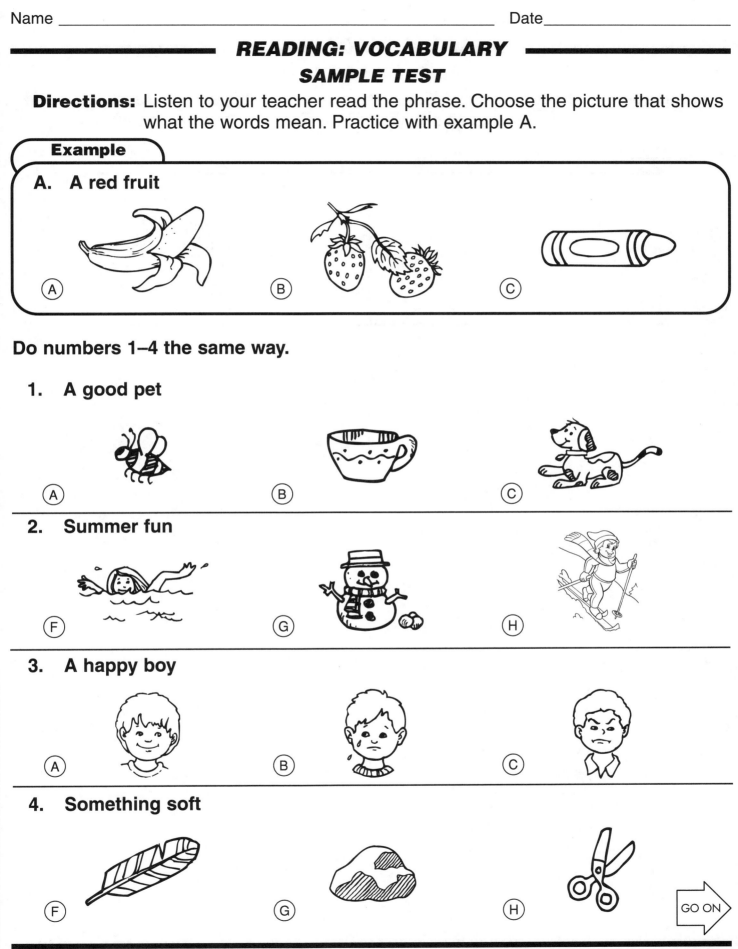

Ⓐ   Ⓑ   Ⓒ

Do numbers 1–4 the same way.

1. **A good pet**

Ⓐ   Ⓑ   Ⓒ

2. **Summer fun**

Ⓕ   Ⓖ   Ⓗ

3. **A happy boy**

Ⓐ   Ⓑ   Ⓒ

4. **Something soft**

Ⓕ   Ⓖ   Ⓗ   GO ON ➡

READING: VOCABULARY
SAMPLE TEST (cont.)

Directions: Look at the picture. Listen as your teacher reads the word choices. Mark the word that goes with the picture. Practice with examples B and C.

Examples

B.
- (F) head
- (G) arm
- (H) hand

C.
- (A) eat
- (B) walk
- (C) wear

Do numbers 5–10 the same way.

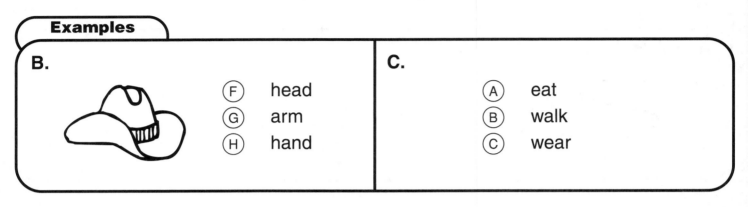

5.
- (A) frog
- (B) turtle
- (C) kitten

6.
- (F) throw
- (G) read
- (H) hold

7.
- (A) girl
- (B) bear
- (C) Santa

8.
- (F) read
- (G) eat
- (H) paint

9.
- (A) bag
- (B) cup
- (C) bowl

10.
- (F) snack
- (G) ice cream
- (H) mud

GO ON

978-1-62057-593-2 *Spectrum Test Practice 1*

READING: VOCABULARY
SAMPLE TEST (cont.)

Directions: Listen to your teacher read the sentence and word choices. Look at the underlined part. Mark the word that means about the same. Do numbers 11–13 the same way.

Directions: Listen to your teacher read the sentence and word choices. Look at the underlined part. Mark the word that is the opposite. Do numbers 14–16 the same way.

11. Brenda was <u>chilly</u>.
- (A) large
- (B) cold
- (C) small
- (D) done

14. Jetta <u>enjoys</u> music.
- (F) hates
- (G) likes
- (H) turns
- (J) eats

12. Bees are <u>insects</u>.
- (F) bugs
- (G) dish
- (H) hat
- (J) tire

15. The lion was <u>huge</u>.
- (A) hungry
- (B) sitting
- (C) small
- (D) fish

13. Levi made a <u>noise</u>.
- (A) flower
- (B) shell
- (C) sound
- (D) stone

16. A turtle is <u>slow</u>.
- (F) lazy
- (G) fun
- (H) tired
- (J) quick

GO ON

READING: VOCABULARY
SAMPLE TEST (cont.)

Directions: Listen to your teacher read the phrases and word choices. Mark the word that matches the phrase. Do numbers 17–19 the same way.

Directions: Listen to your teacher read the sentences and word choices. Mark the word that completes the sentence. Do numbers 20–22 the same way.

17. **a thing we eat...**
   - (A) rope
   - (B) orange
   - (C) pail
   - (D) wheel

18. **a wild animal...**
   - (F) tiger
   - (G) butterfly
   - (H) fly
   - (J) pen

19. **a heavy thing...**
   - (A) feather
   - (B) sock
   - (C) truck
   - (D) balloon

20. **The show was great so we** _____ .
   - (F) clapped
   - (G) swam
   - (H) chewed
   - (J) blinked

21. **I ate the juicy** _____ . **It dripped.**
   - (A) bread
   - (B) stone
   - (C) peach
   - (D) book

22. **Some** _____ **fly south in the winter. It is warm.**
   - (F) bears
   - (G) girls
   - (H) trucks
   - (J) birds

STOP

READING: READING COMPREHENSION

● **Lesson 16: Listening Comprehension**

Directions: Listen to your teacher read each story. Choose the best answer for each question. Practice with example A.

Example

A. Henry Turtle was in a jam. He had been taking his walk when suddenly an owl landed on his head. What a surprise! What was on Henry's head?

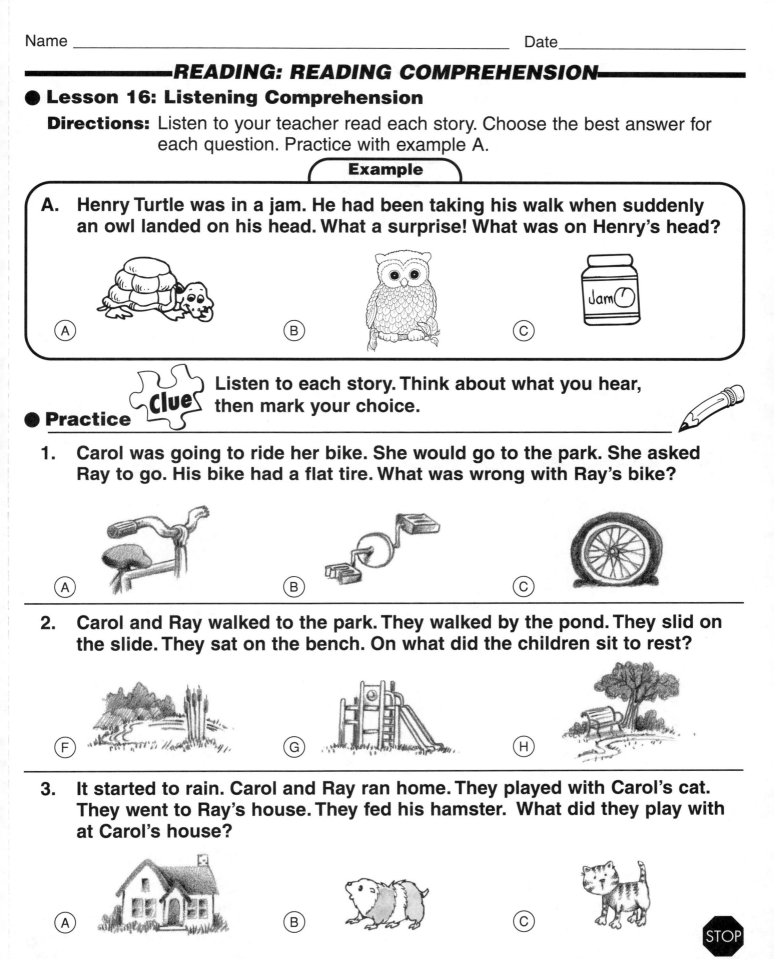

Ⓐ   Ⓑ   Ⓒ

Clue Listen to each story. Think about what you hear, then mark your choice.

● **Practice**

1. Carol was going to ride her bike. She would go to the park. She asked Ray to go. His bike had a flat tire. What was wrong with Ray's bike?

Ⓐ   Ⓑ   Ⓒ

2. Carol and Ray walked to the park. They walked by the pond. They slid on the slide. They sat on the bench. On what did the children sit to rest?

Ⓕ   Ⓖ   Ⓗ

3. It started to rain. Carol and Ray ran home. They played with Carol's cat. They went to Ray's house. They fed his hamster. What did they play with at Carol's house?

Ⓐ   Ⓑ   Ⓒ

STOP

READING: READING COMPREHENSION

● **Lesson 17: Picture Comprehension**

Directions: Look at the picture. Listen to your teacher read the words next to the picture. Mark the choice that best describes the picture. Practice with example A.

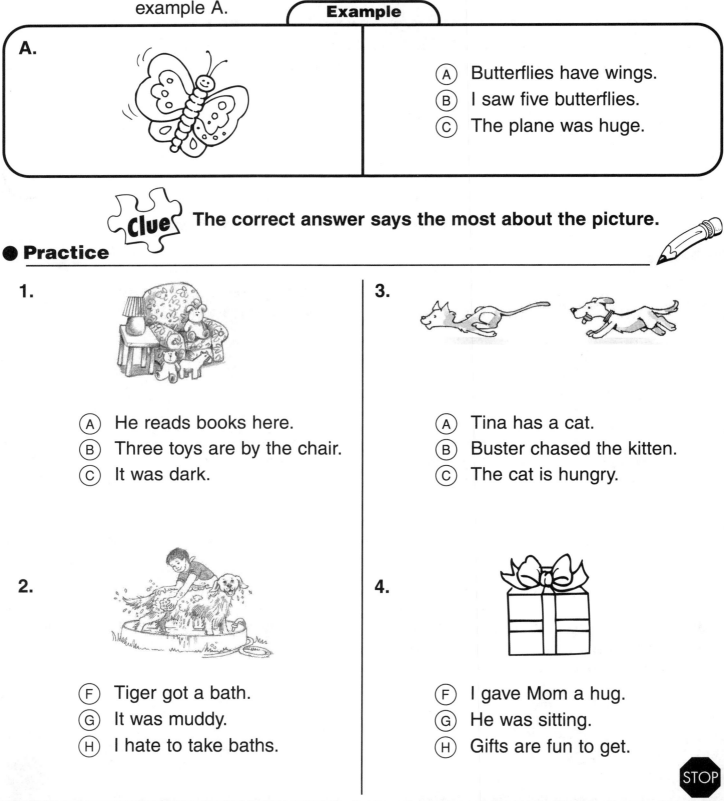

Example

A.
- (A) Butterflies have wings.
- (B) I saw five butterflies.
- (C) The plane was huge.

Clue The correct answer says the most about the picture.

● **Practice**

1.
- (A) He reads books here.
- (B) Three toys are by the chair.
- (C) It was dark.

3.
- (A) Tina has a cat.
- (B) Buster chased the kitten.
- (C) The cat is hungry.

2.
- (F) Tiger got a bath.
- (G) It was muddy.
- (H) I hate to take baths.

4.
- (F) I gave Mom a hug.
- (G) He was sitting.
- (H) Gifts are fun to get.

STOP

READING: READING COMPREHENSION

● **Lesson 18: Sentence Comprehension**

Directions: Listen to your teacher read the sentence. Mark the picture that completes or matches the sentence. Practice with examples A and B.

Examples

A. **This is made of wood. You can write with it.**

Ⓐ   Ⓑ   Ⓒ

B. **I ate a _____.**

Ⓕ book
Ⓖ cookie
Ⓗ mop

Clue Listen to the sentence. Think before you make your choice.

● **Practice**

1. **This is hot. It helps things grow.**

Ⓐ   Ⓑ   Ⓒ

2. **You smell with this. It is on your face.**

Ⓕ   Ⓖ   Ⓗ

3. **This is my _____.**

Ⓐ dog
Ⓑ school
Ⓒ lake

4. **There is a _____ in front of school.**

Ⓕ bike
Ⓖ frog
Ⓗ flag

STOP

READING: READING COMPREHENSION

● **Lesson 19: Fiction**

Directions: Listen to your teacher read the story. Choose the best answers for the questions about the story. Practice with example A.

Example

The boy ran fast. He did not want to be late. Mom was making chicken. It was his favorite food.

A. **What was Mom making?**

Ⓐ shoes

Ⓑ chicken

Ⓒ puddles

Clue Listen carefully to the whole story.

● **Practice**

Steve and his sister were playing. They were in the yard. A bird landed on the fence.

They watched the bird fly to the ground. It picked up some grass. Then it flew to a tree. Steve said the bird was making a nest.

1. **Who was with Steve?**

Ⓐ Steve's mother

Ⓑ Steve's sister

Ⓒ Steve's dog

2. **Where did the bird land?**

Ⓕ on the fence

Ⓖ on the roof

Ⓗ under the tree

READING: READING COMPREHENSION

● **Lesson 20: Fiction**

Directions: Listen to your teacher read the story. Mark the best answers to the questions.

Get Warm

Brenda Butterfly was cold. She did not like it. She liked the sunny, warm weather. But it was autumn. "What can I do to get warm?"

Her friend Buddy knew what to do. "I think you should follow the birds. They fly to warm places in winter."

Brenda liked the idea. "That sounds great! Will you come with me, Buddy?"

They followed a flock of birds. It was a long trip. But it was so warm and sunny! Brenda and Buddy smiled. What a good idea!

There were many butterflies in this place. The flowers were colorful. Maybe Brenda and Buddy would stay.

1. **Brenda did not like _____ .**
   - (A) sunny weather
   - (B) being cold
   - (C) her friend Buddy

2. **What did Buddy think Brenda should do?**
   - (F) follow the birds
   - (G) light a fire
   - (H) get new coats

3. **Why should she follow the birds?**
   - (A) to find water
   - (B) to see snow
   - (C) to get to a warm place

4. **Two things Brenda and Buddy liked now were _____ .**
   - (F) their bird friends and fish
   - (G) colorful flowers and being warm
   - (H) flying far and the moon

READING: READING COMPREHENSION

● **Lesson 21: Reading Literature**

Directions: Listen to your teacher read the story. Mark the best answers to the questions.

Fox and His Trap

One day in the deep, leafy woods, Fox was busy making something. Mouse came by.

"What are you making?" asked Mouse.

"Nothing," answered Fox.

"It looks like a trap to me," said Mouse as she scampered away.

Before long, Duck came by. "What are you making?" asked Duck.

"Nothing," answered Fox.

"It looks like a trap to me," said Duck as he waddled away.

Just as Fox finished, Rabbit came by. "What did you make?" asked Rabbit.

"A cozy home for a rabbit," Fox said.

"It looks like a trap to me," said Rabbit.

"Nonsense," said Fox. "Come closer and have a look."

"I do not think I will fit," said Rabbit.

"Nonsense," said Fox. "It is big enough for me." Fox crawled in. When Fox's bushy red tail was all the way inside, Rabbit shut the latch. The door snapped closed. Rabbit hopped off happily, saying, "It looks like a trap to me."

● **Practice**

1. **How big is the thing Fox makes?**
   - (A) big enough for a fox
   - (B) big enough for a deer
   - (C) big enough for a cow

2. **Who talks to Fox last?**
   - (F) Mouse
   - (G) Duck
   - (H) Rabbit

GO ON

READING: READING COMPREHENSION

● **Lesson 21: Reading Literature (cont.)**

3. **When Rabbit hops off happily, how does Rabbit feel?**

   (A) afraid

   (B) safe

   (C) sad

4. **What word from the story tells how Fox's tail looks?**

   (F) bushy

   (G) busy

   (H) cozy

5. **The reason for this story is to tell about**

   (A) how animals move.

   (B) a fox who is tricked by a rabbit.

   (C) what types of animals a fox eats.

6. **What helps you know the story is not real?**

   (F) The animals talk.

   (G) The animals scamper, waddle, and hop.

   (H) The woods are deep and leafy.

7. **What can you learn from the story?**

   (A) how to build a trap

   (B) how animals move

   (C) how to be careful

8. **Which character is in a happy mood when leaving Fox?**

   (F) Duck

   (G) Rabbit

   (H) Mouse

9. **Why does Fox talk to Rabbit but not Mouse or Duck?**

   (A) because the trap is ready

   (B) because Rabbit is friendly

   (C) because Mouse and Duck are mean

10. **Who tricks whom?**

   (F) Duck tricks Mouse.

   (G) Fox tricks Duck.

   (H) Rabbit tricks Fox.

READING: READING COMPREHENSION

● **Lesson 22: Nonfiction**

Directions: Listen to your teacher read the story. Choose the best answers to the questions about the story.

Spiders

Spiders are animals. The special name for their animal family is "arachnid." One spider is the tarantula. Another is the wolf spider. All spiders have eight legs. Most spiders spin webs of silk. The webs help the spider catch food. They eat mostly insects. Some spiders are big. There is one as big as a man's hand. Some spiders are very small. One spider is as small as the tip of a pin. This animal is helpful to people. Spiders eat harmful or pesky insects. They eat flies and mosquitoes.

1. **Spiders are _____ .**

   (A) insects

   (B) animals

   (C) plants

2. **Spider webs are made of _____ .**

   (F) silk

   (G) rope

   (H) wire

3. **Why are spiders helpful?**

   (A) Spiders are big and small.

   (B) A tarantula is a kind of spider.

   (C) Spiders eat harmful insects.

4. **Why was this story written?**

   (F) to tell about spiders

   (G) to tell about mosquitoes

   (H) to scare you

READING COMPREHENSION

● **Lesson 23: Nonfiction**
Directions: Listen to your teacher read the story. Choose the best answers to the questions.

Statue of Liberty

The Statue of Liberty is in New York. It is a famous statue. People in France gave the United States the statue. This happened in 1884. They wanted to show their friendship.

It is one of the biggest statues ever made. The statue is made from copper. It shows a lady. She is dressed in a robe. She is wearing a crown. The lady is holding a torch and a tablet. A poet wrote a famous poem about the statue. It is on a bronze plaque. People read it when they visit.

Long ago, millions of immigrants, people coming to live in the United States, saw the statue. They felt like she welcomed them. It seemed like her torch was lighting the way to their new home. Millions of other people, called tourists, have also visited. They can climb up to the crown. They can see New York City. Many people around the world know about this great statue.

1. **Who gave the Statue of Liberty to the United States?**
   - (A) the people of France
   - (B) many immigrants
   - (C) the queen

2. **Why did they give the statue to the United States?**
   - (F) to make money
   - (G) so the United States would give them one
   - (H) to show friendship

3. **The statue is made from copper because _____ .**
   - (A) copper is ugly
   - (B) it is strong
   - (C) it smells nice

4. **Immigrants felt like the statue _____ .**
   - (F) worked like a flashlight
   - (G) welcomed them
   - (H) was too tall

READING: READING COMPREHENSION
SAMPLE TEST

Directions: Listen to your teacher read the sentences. Mark the picture that best matches the sentences. Practice with example A. Do numbers 1–3 the same way.

Example

A. **This is my brother. He has glasses.**

Ⓐ   Ⓑ   Ⓒ

1. **Mother grew pretty flowers.**

Ⓐ   Ⓑ   Ⓒ

2. **It is fun at the park. We love to play.**

Ⓕ   Ⓖ   Ⓗ

3. **Kenny loves bears. They are his favorite animal.**

Ⓐ   Ⓑ   Ⓒ

GO ON

━━ READING: READING COMPREHENSION ━━
SAMPLE TEST (cont.)

Directions: Listen to your teacher read the story and the questions. Choose the best answer for each question.

Kite Trouble

The wind was blowing. Inga wanted to fly a kite. It was sunny and warm. She went to the park. Jesse went with her. They ran all the way to the park.

Inga and Jesse got ready. Inga held the kite. Then she held the string. A big wind blew the kite high. Inga ran. Jesse wanted to try. When she stopped running, he asked Inga. Inga gave him the string. A big wind came. The string slipped. The kite went very high. The kite was caught in the tree. Inga and Jesse started to cry. They walked home. Maybe Daddy could help.

4. What did Inga want to do?

　(F) run with Jesse

　(G) fly a kite

　(H) play in the sun

5. What kind of weather was it?

　(A) sunny and warm

　(B) cold and windy

　(C) snowing

6. How did the kite get caught in the tree?

　(F) Daddy put it there.

　(G) Inga ran into the tree.

　(H) A big wind blew it there.

7. Why did Inga and Jesse cry?

　(A) The kite was in the tree.

　(B) It started to rain.

　(C) Jacob broke the kite string.

GO ON

READING: READING COMPREHENSION
SAMPLE TEST (cont.)

Directions: Listen to your teacher read the story and questions. Mark the best answer for the questions.

Apples

Apples grow best where there are four seasons in the year. In the spring, apple trees will have white flowers and small green leaves in their branches. Then the flowers drop off. Tiny green apples start to grow as the weather gets warm. In the summer, the tree branches fill with small apples that grow and grow. In the fall, the big apples are ready to be picked. Leaves start to drop off the branches. In the winter, the apple tree will rest. It does not grow any leaves or apples. It is getting ready to grow blossoms and apples again in the spring.

8. **What grows on the apple tree branches first?**
   - (F) apples
   - (G) bee hives
   - (H) flowers and leaves

9. **In what season do the apples grow and grow?**
   - (A) fall
   - (B) summer
   - (C) winter

10. **What happens to apple trees in the winter?**
    - (F) They rest.
    - (G) They grow very tall.
    - (H) Farmers cut them down.

11. **Why was this story written?**
    - (A) to tell about winter
    - (B) to tell about farming
    - (C) to tell about apples

READING PRACTICE TEST

● **Part 1: Word Analysis**

Directions: Listen to your teacher read each question and the answer choices. Choose the best answer. Practice with example A. Do numbers 1–5 the same way.

Example

A.   Which letter does the word **water** begin with?

  Ⓐ t
  Ⓑ v
  Ⓒ m
  Ⓓ w

1.   Which letter does the word **heart** begin with?

  Ⓐ p
  Ⓑ b
  Ⓒ d
  Ⓓ h

2.   Which letter does the word **take** begin with?

  Ⓕ t
  Ⓖ b
  Ⓗ a
  Ⓙ e

3.   Which letter does the word **sunny** begin with?

  Ⓐ c
  Ⓑ s
  Ⓒ y
  Ⓓ l

4.   Which letter does the word **bottle** begin with?

  Ⓕ d
  Ⓖ h
  Ⓗ b
  Ⓙ p

5.   Which letter does the word **money** begin with?

  Ⓐ m
  Ⓑ n
  Ⓒ w
  Ⓓ j

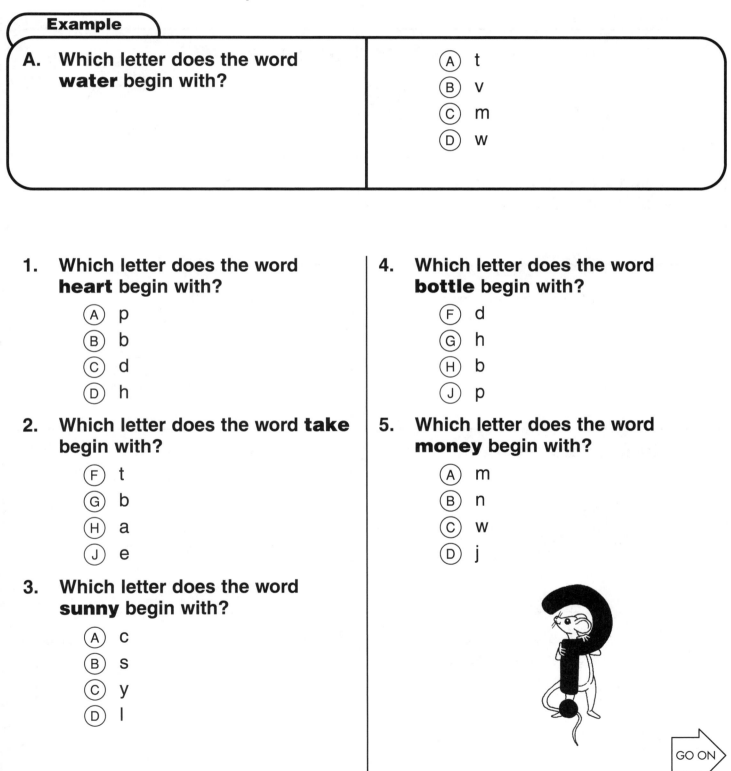

GO ON

Name _____   Date_____

● **Part 1: Word Analysis (cont.)**

Directions: Listen closely as your teacher reads each question and the answer choices. Choose the word with the same beginning or ending sound. Practice with examples B and C. Do the same for numbers 6–9.

Examples

B. **Which picture has the same beginning sound as beet?**

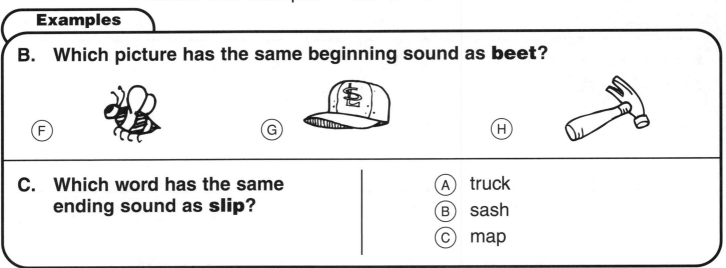

Ⓕ   Ⓖ   Ⓗ

C. **Which word has the same ending sound as slip?**

Ⓐ truck
Ⓑ sash
Ⓒ map

6.   **Which picture has the same beginning sound as cup?**

Ⓕ   Ⓖ   Ⓗ

7.   **Which picture has the same ending sound as Mike?**

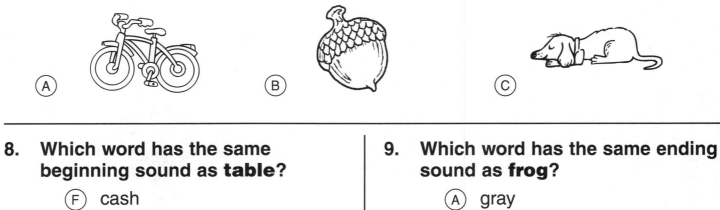

Ⓐ   Ⓑ   Ⓒ

8.   **Which word has the same beginning sound as table?**

Ⓕ cash
Ⓖ shoot
Ⓗ try

9.   **Which word has the same ending sound as frog?**

Ⓐ gray
Ⓑ tag
Ⓒ begin

GO ON

978-1-62057-593-2 *Spectrum Test Practice 1*

Name _____ Date_____

READING PRACTICE TEST

● **Part 1: Word Analysis (cont.)**

Directions: Listen to your teacher say the words. Notice the underlined part. Listen as your teacher reads the word choices. Listen for the word with the same sound as the underlined part and mark it. Practice with example D. Do the same for numbers 10–15.

Example

D. w**i**g

   (F) time

   (G) swam

   (H) tip

10. p**a**t

   (F) from

   (G) mad

   (H) goes

11. m**i**ne

   (A) dime

   (B) into

   (C) hurt

12. p**u**mp

   (F) child

   (G) cutting

   (H) shark

13. sh**ou**t

   (A) loud

   (B) crow

   (C) pill

14. m**a**de

   (F) bank

   (G) puddle

   (H) line

15. b**e**g

   (A) mass

   (B) kelp

   (C) broke

GO ON

978-1-62057-593-2 *Spectrum Test Practice 1*

Name _____ Date_____

READING PRACTICE TEST

● **Part 1: Word Analysis (cont.)**

Directions: Listen to your teacher read the words. Choose the picture that rhymes with the word. Practice with examples E and F. Do the same for numbers 16–19.

Examples

E. **Which picture rhymes with barn?**

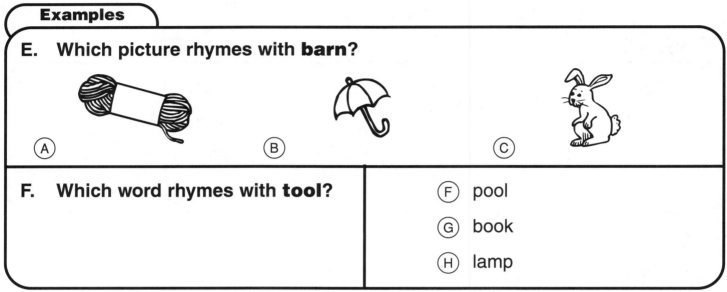

Ⓐ   Ⓑ   Ⓒ

F. **Which word rhymes with tool?**

   Ⓕ pool

   Ⓖ book

   Ⓗ lamp

16. **Which picture rhymes with dish?**

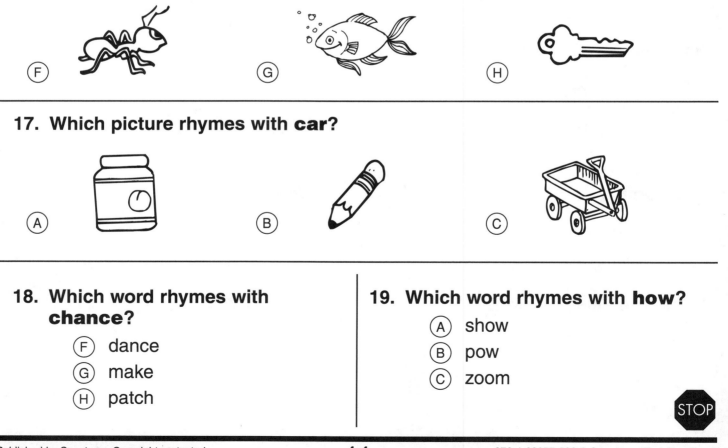

Ⓕ   Ⓖ   Ⓗ

17. **Which picture rhymes with car?**

Ⓐ   Ⓑ   Ⓒ

18. **Which word rhymes with chance?**

   Ⓕ dance

   Ⓖ make

   Ⓗ patch

19. **Which word rhymes with how?**

   Ⓐ show

   Ⓑ pow

   Ⓒ zoom

STOP

READING PRACTICE TEST

● **Part 2: Vocabulary**

Directions: Listen to your teacher read the group of words and answer choices.
Choose the picture that matches the words. Practice with example A.
Do the same for 1–4.

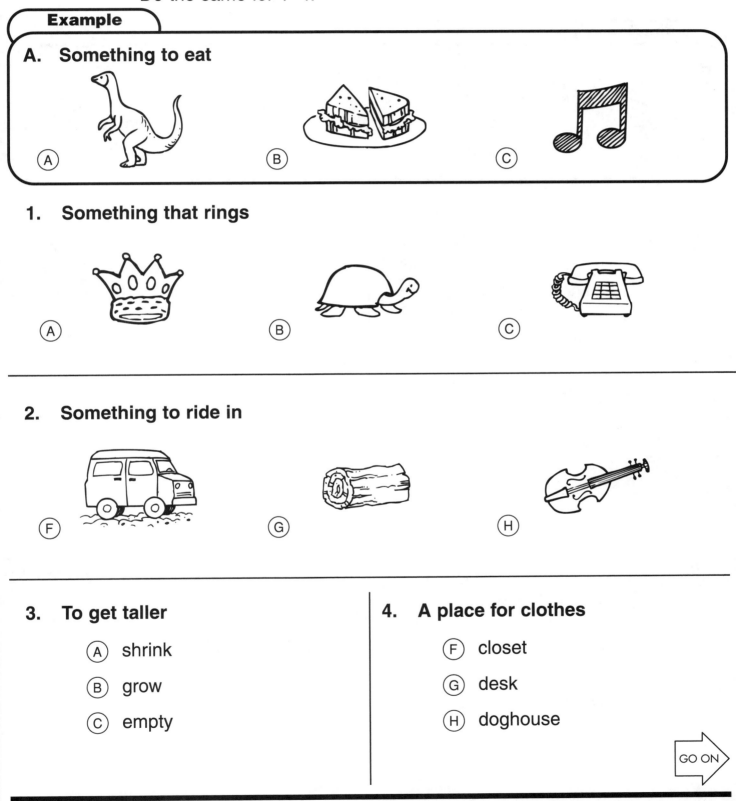

Example

A. Something to eat

Ⓐ   Ⓑ   Ⓒ

1. **Something that rings**

Ⓐ   Ⓑ   Ⓒ

2. **Something to ride in**

Ⓕ   Ⓖ   Ⓗ

3. **To get taller**
   - Ⓐ shrink
   - Ⓑ grow
   - Ⓒ empty

4. **A place for clothes**
   - Ⓕ closet
   - Ⓖ desk
   - Ⓗ doghouse

GO ON

READING PRACTICE TEST

● **Part 2: Vocabulary (cont.)**

Directions: Look at the picture. Listen as your teacher reads the word choices. Mark the word that goes with the picture. Practice with examples B and C. Do the same for numbers 5–12.

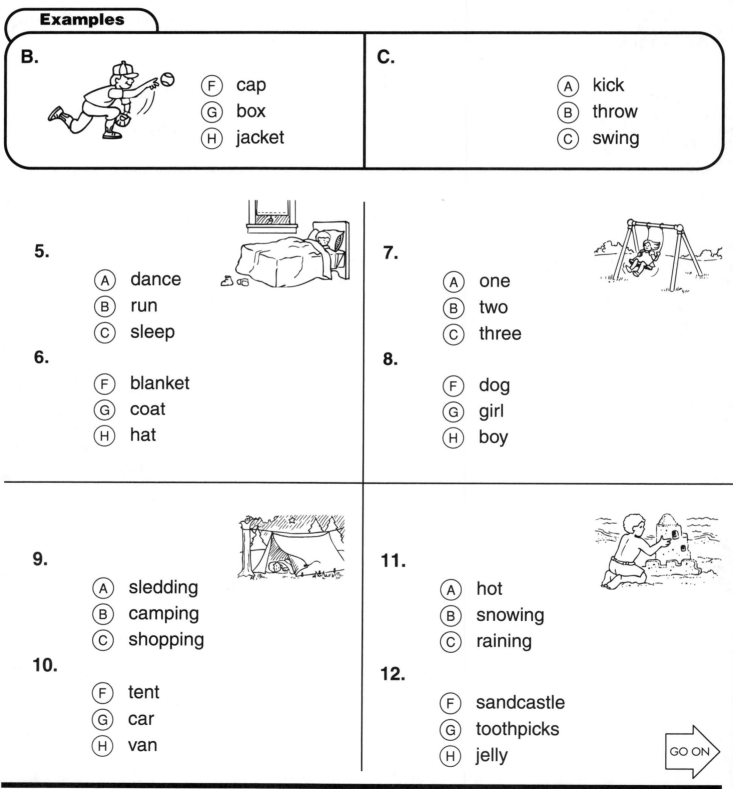

Examples

B.

- (F) cap
- (G) box
- (H) jacket

C.

- (A) kick
- (B) throw
- (C) swing

5.

- (A) dance
- (B) run
- (C) sleep

6.

- (F) blanket
- (G) coat
- (H) hat

7.

- (A) one
- (B) two
- (C) three

8.

- (F) dog
- (G) girl
- (H) boy

9.

- (A) sledding
- (B) camping
- (C) shopping

10.

- (F) tent
- (G) car
- (H) van

11.

- (A) hot
- (B) snowing
- (C) raining

12.

- (F) sandcastle
- (G) toothpicks
- (H) jelly

GO ON

READING PRACTICE TEST

● **Part 2: Vocabulary (cont.)**

Directions: Listen closely as your teacher reads the sentences and word choices. Choose the word that completes the sentence. Practice with example D. Do the same for numbers 13–16.

Example

D. **Camila _____ the phone.**

- (A) ringing
- (B) answered
- (C) went
- (D) shouted

13. **My mother drinks _____ .**

- (A) tea
- (B) nails
- (C) watermelon
- (D) sandwiches

14. **The _____ on the radio was loud.**

- (F) sun
- (G) water
- (H) music
- (J) computer

15. **Lucy walked all the way to the _____ .**

- (A) over
- (B) cut
- (C) jar
- (D) park

16. **Maisie sat on the _____ .**

- (F) touch
- (G) something
- (H) bench
- (J) large

GO ON

Name _____   Date_____

● **Part 2: Vocabulary (cont.)**

Directions: Listen closely as your teacher reads the sentences and word choices. Choose the answer that means the same or about the same as the underlined word for numbers 17–19.

Directions: Listen closely as your teacher reads the sentences and word choices. Choose the answer that means the opposite of the underlined word for numbers 20–22.

17. **Do you <u>like</u> watermelon?**

    (A) make

    (B) enjoy

    (C) hate

    (D) pat

18. **His ideas are always <u>great</u>!**

    (F) wonderful

    (G) crazy

    (H) boring

    (J) bunny

19. **<u>Listen</u> to the story.**

    (A) taste

    (B) hear

    (C) look

    (D) sit

20. **I am <u>wet</u>.**

    (F) soaked

    (G) dry

    (H) yellow

    (J) quiet

21. **Sammy is a <u>tiny</u> mouse.**

    (A) large

    (B) small

    (C) friendly

    (D) brown

22. **The glass is <u>full</u>.**

    (F) mine

    (G) Teri's

    (H) empty

    (J) broken

READING PRACTICE TEST

● **Part 3: Reading Comprehension**

Directions: Listen to your teacher read each story. Choose the best answer for the question. Practice with example A. Do the same for numbers 1–2.

Example

A. Grandfather has a farm. He has many animals. He has pigs, chicks, and horses. He loves pigs the most. Which animal does Grandfather love the most?

Ⓐ   Ⓑ   Ⓒ

1. Katie packed her backpack. She took things to eat. She took things to drink. Which item wouldn't she put in her bag?

Ⓐ   Ⓑ   Ⓒ

2. Lilo was planting a garden. She had many tools. The tools helped her plant. Which picture shows something that Lilo didn't need when planting?

Ⓕ   Ⓖ   Ⓗ

GO ON

978-1-62057-593-2 *Spectrum Test Practice 1*

READING PRACTICE TEST

● **Part 3: Reading Comprehension (cont.)**

Directions: Listen to your teacher read the sentences. Look at the pictures. Choose the sentence that matches the picture. Practice with example B. Do 3–6 the same way.

Example

B.

Ⓕ Todd ate cereal.

Ⓖ I love my horse.

Ⓗ The weather is nice.

3.

Ⓐ The boat sunk.

Ⓑ My pen does not work.

Ⓒ Tanika swims every day.

4.

Ⓕ Lee gave him a car.

Ⓖ My dad has a new watch.

Ⓗ I see the clock.

5.

Ⓐ We read together.

Ⓑ I ran away from my brother.

Ⓒ He plays the flute.

6.

Ⓕ It was snowing.

Ⓖ Parker was singing.

Ⓗ I go to the library.

GO ON

READING PRACTICE TEST

● **Part 3: Reading Comprehension (cont.)**

Directions: Listen to your teacher read the sentences. Match a picture to the sentences. Practice with example C. Do the same for numbers 7–10.

Example

C. **This floats high. Some people ride them.**

7. **It was very cold. Mother said to wear these.**

8. **It was time. We had to get there fast!**

9. **One boy is _____ .**
   - (A) whispering
   - (B) jumping
   - (C) eating

10. **One boy is _____ .**
   - (F) listening
   - (G) awake
   - (H) sleeping

GO ON

978-1-62057-593-2 *Spectrum Test Practice 1*

READING PRACTICE TEST

● **Part 3: Reading Comprehension (cont.)**

Directions: Listen to your teacher read the story and the questions. Choose the best answer to the questions. Practice with example D. Do the same for numbers 11–14.

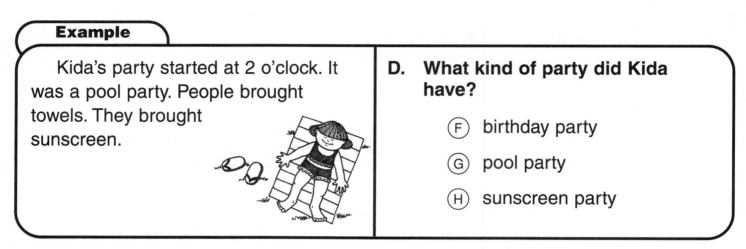

Example

Kida's party started at 2 o'clock. It was a pool party. People brought towels. They brought sunscreen.

D. What kind of party did Kida have?

F birthday party

G pool party

H sunscreen party

The box was heavy. Simon needed help to move it. He asked Tom. He asked Kate. They went to help. The box was full. It had books in it. Tom and Kate decided to read. Simon sat down to read too. The box stayed.

11. What was in the box?

A Simon

B books

C boxes

12. How many people came to help Simon?

F 1

G 2

H 3

13. What did Tom and Kate do?

A read books

B moved the box

C ran away

14. Why didn't they move the box?

F It was purple.

G They wanted to read.

H Kate went home.

GO ON

Name _____ Date_____

● **Part 3: Reading Comprehension (cont.)**
Directions: Listen to your teacher read the story and the questions. Choose the best answer to the questions. Do the same for numbers 15–18.

Riley's Racer

"I want to make a car," Riley said to his father. "Will you help?"

"Yes! We can make a car. We need a plan. We need the tools. Then we will buy the things we need to make it."

Riley and his father drew a plan for the car. They decided on the size and color. Riley was so happy! It would be big! He could sit in it. It would roll down the hill in the yard. He would wear a helmet.

It took two weeks to make. They had fun. Mom took pictures. She even helped paint the car red. It was a fun family project.

15. What did Riley want to make?

   (A) tools

   (B) a car

   (C) pictures

16. What did they do first?

   (F) made a plan

   (G) painted

   (H) wore a helmet

17. Why would Riley wear a helmet when riding in the car?

   (A) to be safe

   (B) to hide his hair

   (C) to show his friend

18. How did the family feel?

   (F) sad

   (G) happy

   (H) angry

GO ON ⟩

READING PRACTICE TEST

● **Part 3: Reading Comprehension (cont.)**

Directions: Listen to your teacher read the story and the questions. Choose the best answer to the question. Do the same for numbers 19–22.

Ship Shape

A ship is a very large boat. It can travel in the ocean. Some take trips across the whole ocean. Ships carry people and things from one place to another. They have people to work on them. These workers are called the crew.

A ship has many parts. The stern is the back of the ship. The bow is the front. On some ships masts hold the sails. The sails are like big sheets. They catch the wind and help ships go fast. Up on the mast might be a crow's nest. A sailor can sit there. He can watch the ocean.

Another important part is the helm. This is the ship's steering wheel. It can turn the ship to the left and right.

19. What is a ship?

   Ⓐ a train

   Ⓑ a very large boat

   Ⓒ a raft

20. Where do many ships travel?

   Ⓕ across the ocean

   Ⓖ in rivers

   Ⓗ to dark places

21. What do sails do?

   Ⓐ carry people

   Ⓑ cover people

   Ⓒ help the ship go

22. Why did the author write this story?

   Ⓕ to tell about sailors

   Ⓖ to tell about ships

   Ⓗ so people would buy boats

GO ON

READING PRACTICE TEST

● **Part 3: Reading Comprehension (cont.)**

Directions: Listen to your teacher read the story and the questions. Choose the best answer to the question. Do the same for numbers 23–26.

What About Rabbits?

Rabbits are small animals. They have short, fluffy tails. Some have long ears that can hear very well. These ears can be floppy. Some also stick right up!

Rabbits eat all kinds of plants. They eat in fields. They eat in gardens. Some farmers do not like rabbits. They eat the vegetables farmers grow. Sometimes the rabbits eat young trees.

When a mother rabbit is having babies, she digs a hole. She puts in soft grass. She adds her own fur. This will keep the babies warm. She may have two to ten babies. Baby rabbits are called kits.

Some people have pet rabbits. They keep them in pens or cages. They might enter them in contests. Some pet rabbits can be trained to do tricks. Grains, vegetables, and grass are good foods for them.

23. What is this story mostly about?
- (A) rabbits
- (B) plants rabbits eat
- (C) farming

24. Why do some farmers not like rabbits?
- (F) They run on the grass.
- (G) They eat their trees and vegetables.
- (H) They make too much noise.

25. Where might pet rabbits sleep?
- (A) in a field
- (B) a pen or cage
- (C) under the blanket

26. What are good foods for pet rabbits?
- (F) vegetables and grass
- (G) hot dogs and candy
- (H) vegetables and meat

STOP

Name _____   Date _____

LANGUAGE: LISTENING

● Lesson 1: Listening Skills

Directions: Listen to your teacher read each story. Then choose the best answer for the question. Practice with example A.

Example

A. Mr. Turner is a teacher. He uses special tools. What is something that he uses?

Ⓐ   Ⓑ   Ⓒ

● **Practice** **Clue** Listen carefully to the whole story and question. Then choose your answer.

1. It was raining. I stayed in the house. I read books. Then I made cookies with Mother. It was a good day. What did I do first?

Ⓐ   Ⓑ   Ⓒ

2. Marco likes to paint. He paints pictures of animals. At school he painted a picture of a parrot. The teacher liked it. The picture is hanging in the classroom. What animal did Marco paint at school?

Ⓕ   Ⓖ   Ⓗ

3. Jamal went to the beach. He found three shells on Monday. He found five shells on Tuesday. On Wednesday, he found two more. How many shells did he find on Tuesday?

Ⓐ   Ⓑ   Ⓒ

GO ON

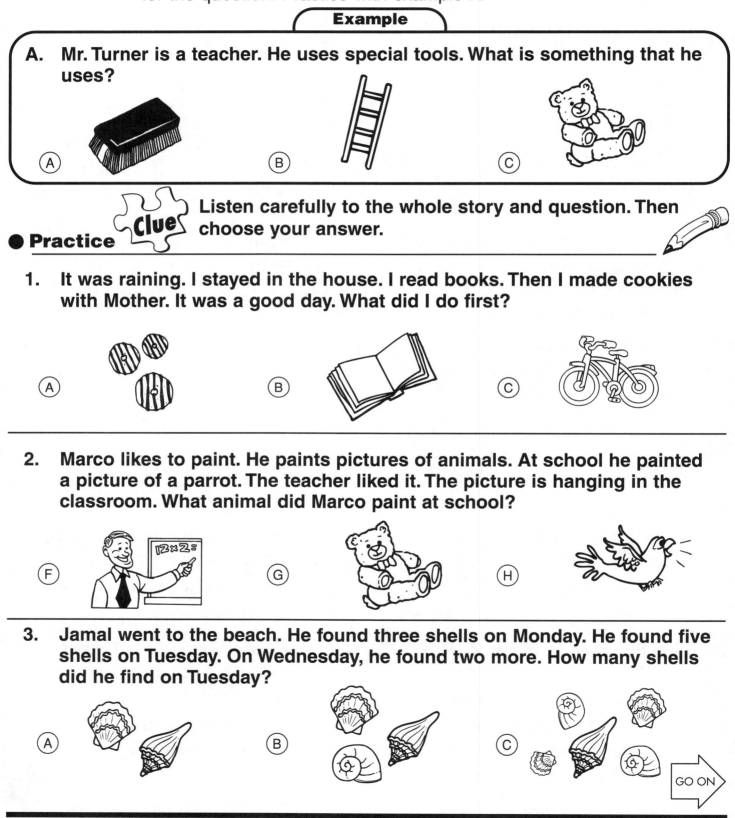

Name _____ Date_____

● **Lesson 1: Listening Skills (cont.)**

4. The cat was meowing. She wanted to eat. Betty had no cat food! Lydia said she would go to the store. She would buy it. Maybe she would buy treats too. Where would Lydia go?

Ⓕ   Ⓖ   Ⓗ

5. Juan was playing. He has a soccer ball in the house. Mom said, "No kicking." But Juan kicked! The ball hit Mom's vase. It broke. Juan told Mom. They fixed it together. What broke?

Ⓐ   Ⓑ   Ⓒ

6. Uncle Timothy is very tall. He plays a sport. He wears a blue and white shirt and shorts. He throws a ball. The people clap when it goes in the basket. He makes many points. Which sport does Uncle Timothy play?

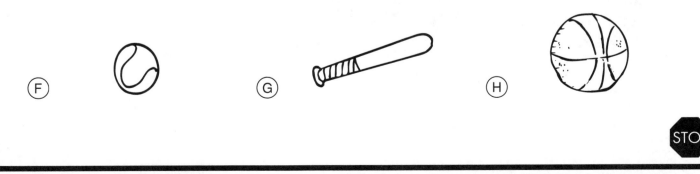

Ⓕ   Ⓖ   Ⓗ

STOP

Name _____   Date _____

LANGUAGE: LISTENING

● Lesson 2: Listening Skills

Directions: Listen to your teacher read the sentences. Then choose the best answer to complete each story. Practice with examples A and B.

Examples

A. Dogs make good pets. Most are friendly. They like to play. You can train a dog. Dogs make _____ .

- (A) good pets
- (B) dinner
- (C) plants grow

B. Tina was happy. It was her dad's birthday. She made a card. Mom made a cake. They would sing. They would eat the _____ .

- (F) card
- (G) cake
- (H) birthday gift

● Practice

1. Rudy had one dollar. He used it to buy a book. It was about bugs. Rudy went home to read. He sat by the tree. Rudy read about _____ .

- (A) trees
- (B) dollars
- (C) bugs

2. They set up camp. Sam put up the tent. Kyle dug a hole. Father built a campfire. They cooked hot dogs. Later they told stories. It was time to sleep. Father told one more story. The boys snored loudly in the tent. The family set up _____ .

- (F) a table
- (G) camp
- (H) the baseball game

3. Where did the boys sleep?

- (A) in the tent
- (B) next to the lake
- (C) in the kitchen

4. The phone rang. It was Grandmother. She needed help. Her cat ran away. Jack went on his bike. The cat was up a tree. She was meowing. Jack climbed up the tree and got her. She was happy to be down. Grandmother was happy too. Grandmother called _____ for help.

- (F) the cat
- (G) Jack
- (H) a dog

5. Why was she happy?

- (A) The cat was meowing.
- (B) Jack got the cat.
- (C) She took Jack's bike.

STOP

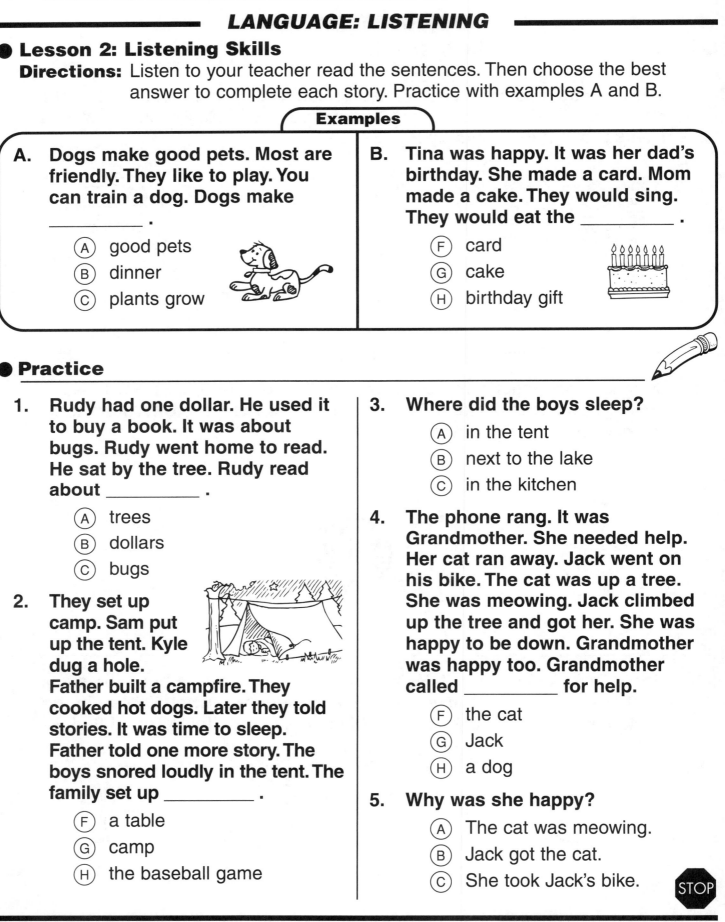

Name _____   Date _____

LANGUAGE: LISTENING

● **Lesson 3: Language Skills**

Directions: Listen to your teacher read the story. Mark the choice that best answers the question. Practice with example A.

Example

A. Mikkel plays baseball. What might he need to play?

Ⓐ   Ⓑ   Ⓒ

Clue If you are not sure which answer is correct, take your best guess.

● **Practice**

1. Tomas loves to watch planes. He goes to the airport. What does he use to see the planes?

Ⓐ   Ⓑ   Ⓒ

2. The weather is hot. What does Petra need to keep cool?

Ⓕ   Ⓖ   Ⓗ

3. Mark is going to the zoo. He will take some pictures. What will he take with him?

Ⓐ   Ⓑ   Ⓒ

GO ON

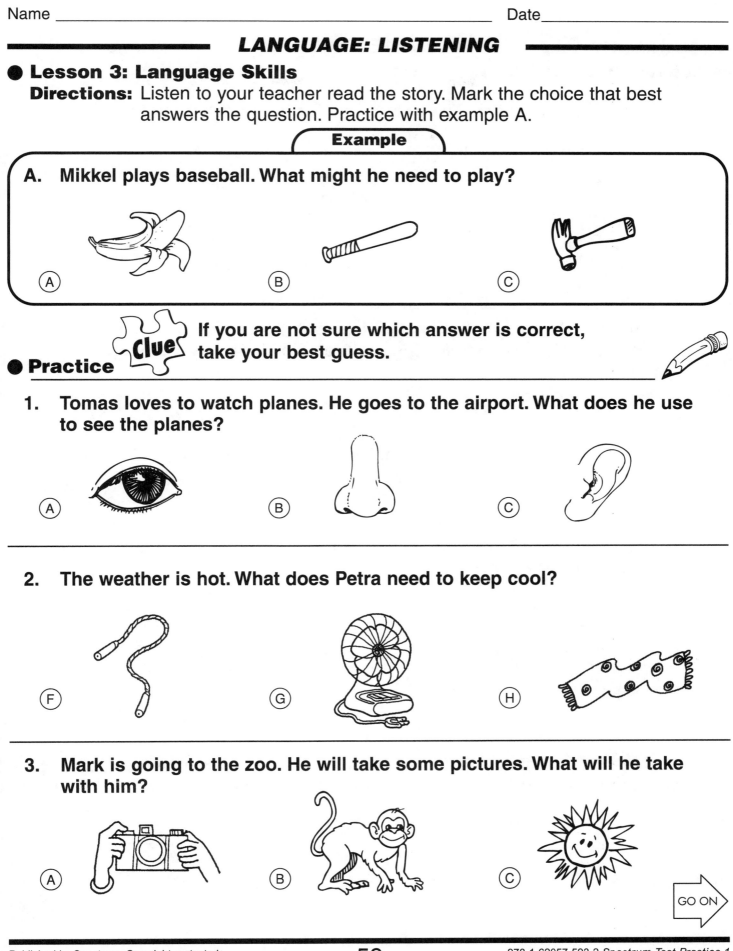

LANGUAGE: LISTENING

● **Lesson 3: Language Skills (cont.)**

4. It was fun at the beach. The girls swam for hours. What did they wear?

Ⓕ   Ⓖ   Ⓗ

5. Some animals are small. A mouse is small. Other animals are big. An elephant is big. Of the following pictures which shows the biggest animal?

Ⓐ   Ⓑ   Ⓒ

6. We will visit Aunt Tina. She lives very far away. We want to get there fast. How should we travel?

Ⓕ   Ⓖ   Ⓗ

7. Arthur built a clubhouse. It was in a tree. It was made of wood. He hung a sign. It said, "No girls can come in!" Who was upset about the sign?

Ⓐ   Ⓑ   Ⓒ   STOP

Name _____   Date_____

LANGUAGE: LISTENING
SAMPLE TEST

Directions: Listen to your teacher read each story. Mark the best answer to the question. Practice with example A. Do numbers 1–6 the same way.

Example

A. **Our neighbor has a garden. He grows vegetables. The vegetables are delicious. He grows corn and beans. He grows lettuce and tomatoes. What might be growing in the garden?**

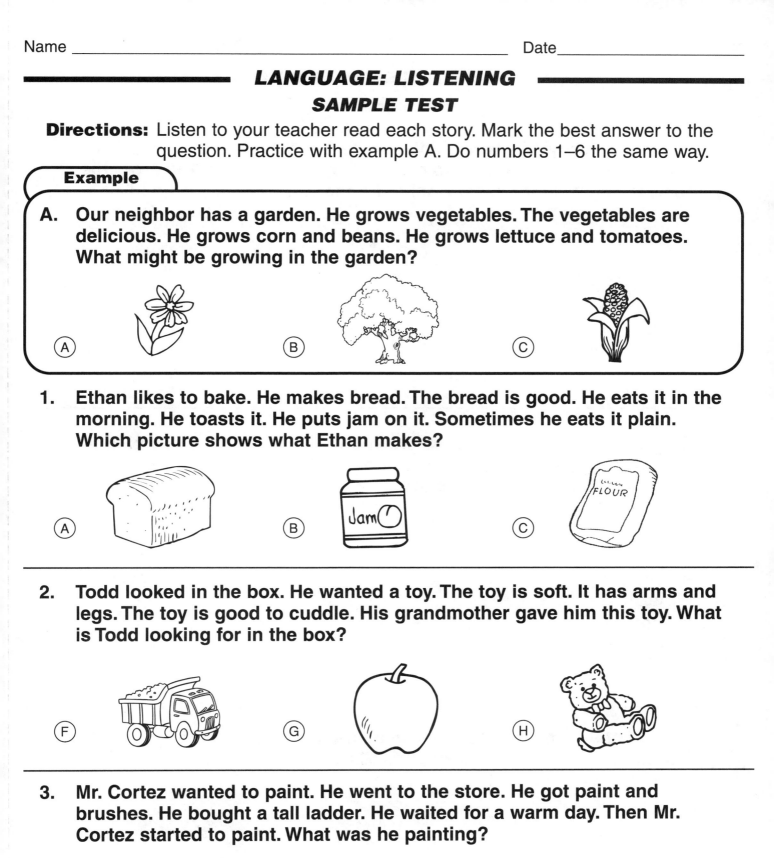

Ⓐ   Ⓑ   Ⓒ

1. **Ethan likes to bake. He makes bread. The bread is good. He eats it in the morning. He toasts it. He puts jam on it. Sometimes he eats it plain. Which picture shows what Ethan makes?**

Ⓐ   Ⓑ   Ⓒ

2. **Todd looked in the box. He wanted a toy. The toy is soft. It has arms and legs. The toy is good to cuddle. His grandmother gave him this toy. What is Todd looking for in the box?**

Ⓕ   Ⓖ   Ⓗ

3. **Mr. Cortez wanted to paint. He went to the store. He got paint and brushes. He bought a tall ladder. He waited for a warm day. Then Mr. Cortez started to paint. What was he painting?**

Ⓐ   Ⓑ   Ⓒ   GO ON

978-1-62057-593-2 *Spectrum Test Practice 1*

4. Anita was ready. She was going to race. There were many people at the race. All the people were in a group. They ran fast. But Anita was the fastest! She won the race. What did Anita win?

(F)   (G)   (H)

5. Grandfather tells stories. They are about family. His family lived in the mountains. They lived near the woods. They had a farm and grew food. They also had many animals. Which animal might have been on the farm?

(A)   (B)   (C)

6. The weatherman said there would be thunder. He said there would be lightning. He said to bring an umbrella. Mother said to bring a jacket. What was the weather?

(F)   (G)   (H)

GO ON

LANGUAGE: LISTENING
SAMPLE TEST (cont.)

Directions: Listen to your teacher read each story. Listen to the answer choices. Mark the best answer to the question. Practice with examples B and C. Do 7–10 the same way.

Examples

B. Jesse had money. He needed milk. He ran fast. He wanted to get there quick. It would close soon. Where was Jesse going?

- (F) to the store
- (G) to school
- (H) to Grandmother's house

C. This is a good pet. Many people have this animal. It purrs. It meows. It chases mice. What kind of animal is it?

- (A) a kangaroo
- (B) a cat
- (C) a hamster

7. Penguins are birds. Most penguins live where it is cold and icy. They love to swim. They are fast swimmers. They have flippers that help them move fast. They can also slide! Sometimes they need to go fast. Swimming and sliding are two ways they go fast. Penguins slide on _____ .

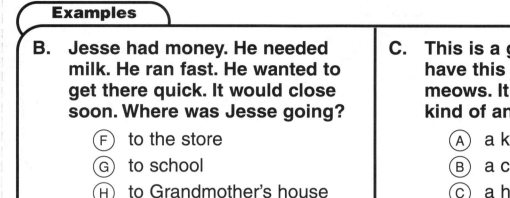

- (A) bananas
- (B) ice
- (C) water

8. When penguins swim their flippers _____ .

- (F) help them move fast
- (G) turn yellow
- (H) turn into ice cubes

9. I open the door. I see balloons and streamers. I hear people laughing and talking. I see a big cake. There are candles on it. There is a big table. It has many boxes on it. The boxes are all colors and shapes. Someone sees me. Everyone says,

_____ .

- (A) "Go away!"
- (B) "Happy Birthday!"
- (C) "You are silly."

10. The colorful boxes are _____ .

- (F) for the trash
- (G) in the freezer
- (H) birthday gifts

STOP

LANGUAGE: LANGUAGE MECHANICS

● **Lesson 4: Capitalization**

Directions: Listen to your teacher read each sentence. Which word in the sentence needs to be capitalized? If no more capital letters are needed, choose none. Practice with examples A and B.

Examples

A. My cat's name is bill.
- (A) Cat's
- (B) Name
- (C) Bill
- (D) None

B. the flower was pink and white.
- (F) The
- (G) Flower
- (H) White
- (J) None

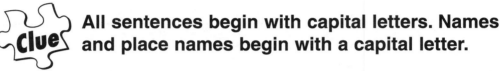

Clue All sentences begin with capital letters. Names and place names begin with a capital letter.

● **Practice**

1. School starts at 8:30.
- (A) Starts
- (B) At
- (C) 8:30
- (D) None

2. Her sister lives in michigan.
- (F) Sister
- (G) Lives
- (H) Michigan
- (J) None

3. May i go to the park?
- (A) I
- (B) Go
- (C) Park
- (D) None

4. We went on monday.
- (F) Went
- (G) On
- (H) Monday
- (J) None

STOP

64 978-1-62057-593-2 *Spectrum Test Practice 1*

■ LANGUAGE: LANGUAGE MECHANICS ■

● Lesson 5: Capitalization

Directions: Listen to your teacher read each story. Look at the underlined part. Think about how it should be written. Choose the best answer. Practice with example A. Do numbers 1–2 the same way.

Directions: Listen to your teacher read each sentence. Think about which word needs a capital letter. Choose the best answer. Practice with example B. Do numbers 3–5 the same way.

Examples

A. We got a new dog. We named

her <u>cotton candy</u>. She is gold
    (A)
and brown.

  (A) cotton Candy

  (B) Cotton Candy

  (C) No change

B. Jack ran with tommy.

  (F) Ran

  (G) With

  (H) Tommy

The Race

We ran in a race. It was on

<u>Saturday, april 10</u>. We went down
      (1)
<u>main Street</u>. Then we turned on
   (2)
Jackson. Timmy won!

1. How should the day of the race be written?

  (A) Saturday, April 10

  (B) saturday, April 10

  (C) No change

2. How should the name of the first street be written?

  (F) Main street

  (G) Main Street

  (H) No change

3. We start school on monday.

  (A) Start

  (B) School

  (C) Monday

4. we saw a bear.

  (F) We

  (G) Saw

  (H) Bear

5. She lives in washington.

  (A) Lives

  (B) In

  (C) Washington

STOP

LANGUAGE: LANGUAGE MECHANICS

● Lesson 6: Punctuation

Directions: Listen to your teacher read the sentences. Some may need punctuation at the end. Choose the correct punctuation mark. If none is needed, mark None. Practice with examples A and B.

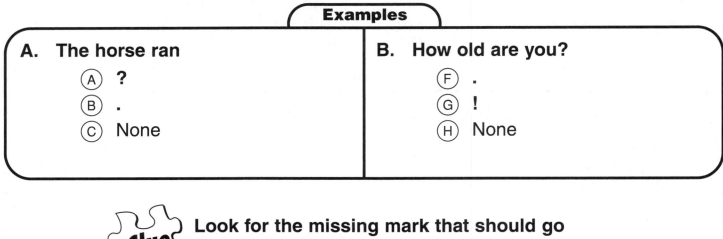

Examples

A. The horse ran

- Ⓐ ?
- Ⓑ .
- Ⓒ None

B. How old are you?

- Ⓕ .
- Ⓖ !
- Ⓗ None

Clue Look for the missing mark that should go at the end of the sentences.

● Practice

1. I like peanut butter

- Ⓐ .
- Ⓑ ?
- Ⓒ None

2. Can Tish come over

- Ⓕ .
- Ⓖ ?
- Ⓗ None

3. That is so huge

- Ⓐ ?
- Ⓑ !
- Ⓒ None

4. Harvey caught a fish

- Ⓕ .
- Ⓖ ?
- Ⓗ None

5. May I have more

- Ⓐ .
- Ⓑ ?
- Ⓒ None

6. That is amazing

- Ⓕ !
- Ⓖ ?
- Ⓗ None

STOP

Published by Spectrum. Copyright protected.   978-1-62057-593-2 *Spectrum Test Practice 1*

LANGUAGE: LANGUAGE MECHANICS

● Lesson 7: Punctuation

Directions: Listen to your teacher read each sentence. Does it need a punctuation mark? Choose the correct punctuation. Practice with example A. Do 1 and 2 the same way.

Directions: Listen to your teacher read the sentences and the questions. Choose the correct answer. Practice with example B. Do 3–4 the same way.

Examples

A. I read the book (A) It was long.

- (A) book?
- (B) book.
- (C) book!

B. This is a good cake

What punctuation mark comes after cake?

- (F) cake?
- (G) cake.
- (H) cake!

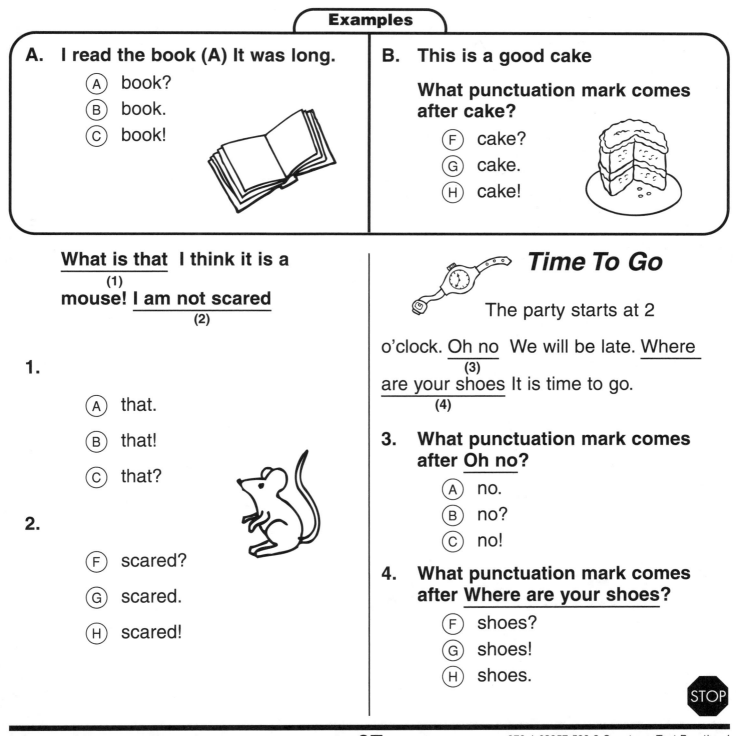

What is that I think it is a
   (1)
mouse! I am not scared
   (2)

1.

- (A) that.
- (B) that!
- (C) that?

2.

- (F) scared?
- (G) scared.
- (H) scared!

Time To Go

The party starts at 2 o'clock. Oh no We will be late. Where
   (3)
are your shoes It is time to go.
   (4)

3. **What punctuation mark comes after Oh no?**

- (A) no.
- (B) no?
- (C) no!

4. **What punctuation mark comes after Where are your shoes?**

- (F) shoes?
- (G) shoes!
- (H) shoes.

STOP

LANGUAGE: LANGUAGE MECHANICS

● Lesson 8: Capitalization and Punctuation

Directions: Listen to your teacher read the sentences. Look at each closely. Choose the sentence that has the correct punctuation and capitalization. Practice with examples A and B.

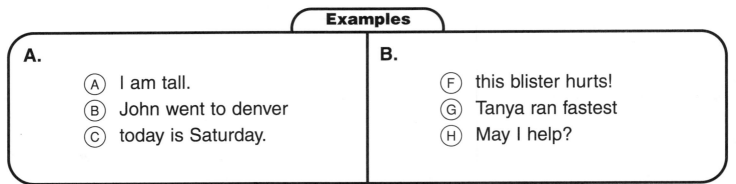

Examples

A.

- Ⓐ I am tall.
- Ⓑ John went to denver
- Ⓒ today is Saturday.

B.

- Ⓕ this blister hurts!
- Ⓖ Tanya ran fastest
- Ⓗ May I help?

 Clue Remember, you are looking for correct punctuation and capitalization.

● Practice

1.
- Ⓐ You are nice
- Ⓑ george has short hair.
- Ⓒ Andy is my friend.

2.
- Ⓕ The Dog barked.
- Ⓖ Where is Daddy?
- Ⓗ Stop that yelling

3.
- Ⓐ i went on Sunday.
- Ⓑ Lydia left on Friday
- Ⓒ Monday was hot!

4.
- Ⓕ The Box is brown.
- Ⓖ the baby was cute.
- Ⓗ My pool is deep.

5.
- Ⓐ Don't open that!
- Ⓑ I hit the Ball?
- Ⓒ Kyle found four leaves

6.
- Ⓕ The joke was Funny!
- Ⓖ We laughed.
- Ⓗ May i have some water?

 STOP

Name _____ Date _____

LANGUAGE: LANGUAGE MECHANICS
SAMPLE TEST

Directions: Listen to your teacher read each sentence. Which word in the sentence needs to be capitalized? If no more capital letters are needed, choose None. Practice with example A. Do numbers 1–6 the same way.

Example

A. **The phone on the desk rang.**

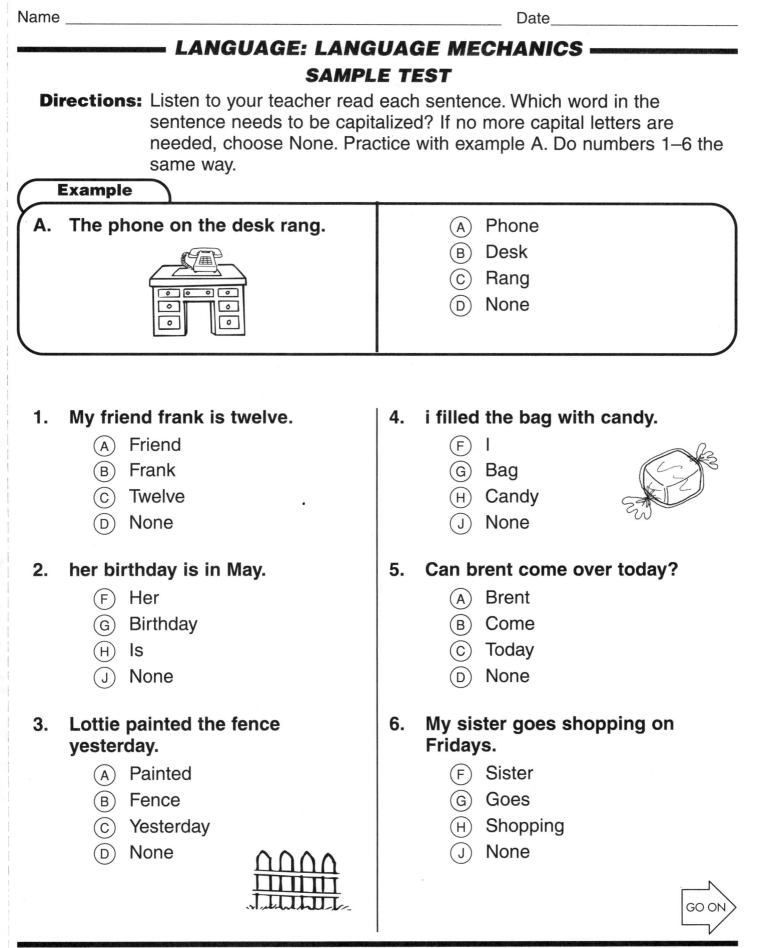

  Ⓐ Phone
  Ⓑ Desk
  Ⓒ Rang
  Ⓓ None

1. **My friend frank is twelve.**
  Ⓐ Friend
  Ⓑ Frank
  Ⓒ Twelve
  Ⓓ None

2. **her birthday is in May.**
  Ⓕ Her
  Ⓖ Birthday
  Ⓗ Is
  Ⓙ None

3. **Lottie painted the fence yesterday.**
  Ⓐ Painted
  Ⓑ Fence
  Ⓒ Yesterday
  Ⓓ None

4. **i filled the bag with candy.**
  Ⓕ I
  Ⓖ Bag
  Ⓗ Candy
  Ⓙ None

5. **Can brent come over today?**
  Ⓐ Brent
  Ⓑ Come
  Ⓒ Today
  Ⓓ None

6. **My sister goes shopping on Fridays.**
  Ⓕ Sister
  Ⓖ Goes
  Ⓗ Shopping
  Ⓙ None

GO ON

978-1-62057-593-2 *Spectrum Test Practice 1*

Name _____ Date _____

LANGUAGE: LANGUAGE MECHANICS
SAMPLE TEST (cont.)

Directions: Listen to your teacher read each story and the questions. Choose the best answer. Practice with examples B and C. Then do 7–10 the same way.

I wrote <u>a Letter</u>. It was to my uncle. I told him about <u>Camp froggy</u>.
      (B)   (C)

B. How should (B) be written?

    (F) a letter

    (G) A letter

    (H) The way it is.

C. How should (C) be written?

    (A) camp Froggy

    (B) Camp Froggy

    (C) The way it is.

Kittens for Free

There was a big sign. <u>it said</u>, "Free Kittens." I asked <u>mom</u>. She
                        (1)   (2)
said to ask Dad. It was fine with him. We named the kitten <u>Sonny</u>.
                                                             (3)
He liked to drink <u>Milk</u>.
                    (4)

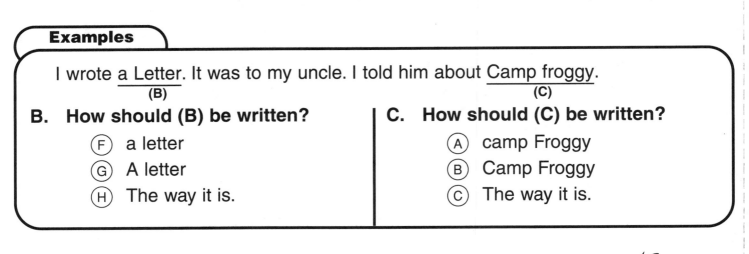

7. **How should the first underlined part be written?**

    (A) It Said,

    (B) It said,

    (C) The way it is.

8. **How should the second underlined part be written?**

    (F) Mom

    (G) MOM

    (H) The way it is.

9. **How should the next underlined part be written?**

    (A) Son Ny

    (B) sonny

    (C) The way it is.

10. **How should the last underlined part be written?**

    (F) milk

    (G) miLk

    (H) The way it is.

GO ON

Name _____   Date_____

LANGUAGE: LANGUAGE MECHANICS
SAMPLE TEST (cont.)

Directions: Listen to your teacher read each sentence. Choose the correct punctuation mark. If the sentence does not need punctuation, choose None. Practice with example D. Do 11–16 the same way.

Example

D. The feather is soft

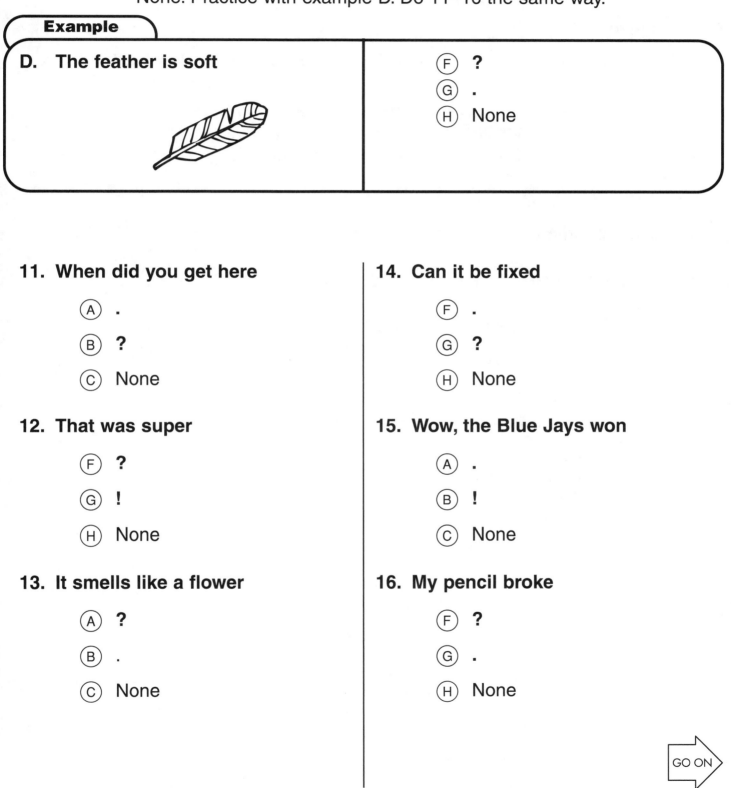

    (F) ?

    (G) .

    (H) None

11. **When did you get here**

    (A) .

    (B) ?

    (C) None

12. **That was super**

    (F) ?

    (G) !

    (H) None

13. **It smells like a flower**

    (A) ?

    (B) .

    (C) None

14. **Can it be fixed**

    (F) .

    (G) ?

    (H) None

15. **Wow, the Blue Jays won**

    (A) .

    (B) !

    (C) None

16. **My pencil broke**

    (F) ?

    (G) .

    (H) None

GO ON

978-1-62057-593-2 *Spectrum Test Practice 1*

LANGUAGE: LANGUAGE MECHANICS
SAMPLE TEST (cont.)

Directions: Listen to your teacher read the story. Look at the underlined part. If it needs punctuation, choose the correct punctuation mark. Practice with example E. Do 17–20 the same way.

Example

The hot dog fell. I was very sad. <u>It was my dinner</u>
(E)

E. What punctuation mark comes after It was my dinner?

- Ⓐ dinner?
- Ⓑ dinner.
- Ⓒ dinner!

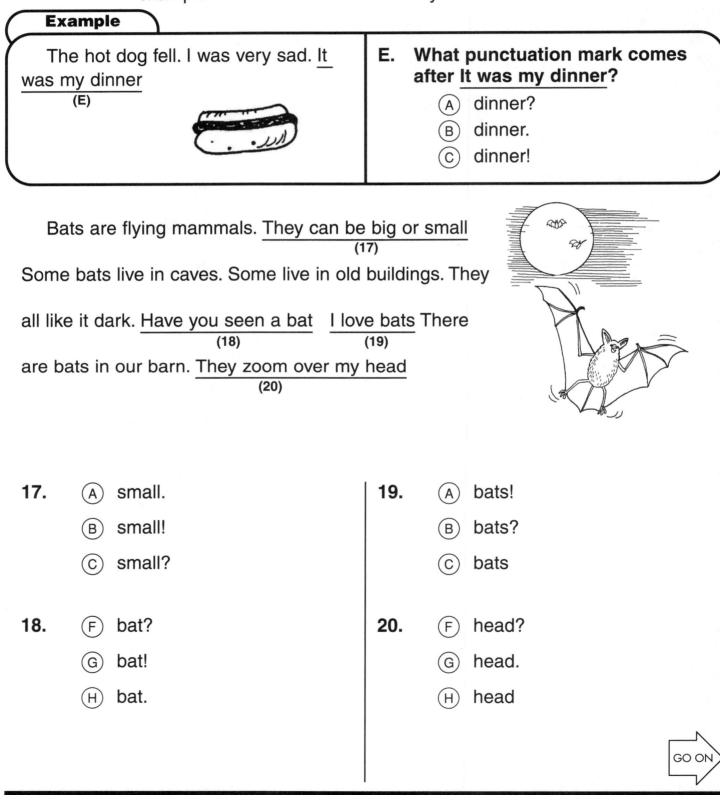

Bats are flying mammals. <u>They can be big or small</u>
(17)

Some bats live in caves. Some live in old buildings. They

all like it dark. <u>Have you seen a bat</u>   <u>I love bats</u> There
(18)   (19)

are bats in our barn. <u>They zoom over my head</u>
(20)

17.
- Ⓐ small.
- Ⓑ small!
- Ⓒ small?

18.
- Ⓕ bat?
- Ⓖ bat!
- Ⓗ bat.

19.
- Ⓐ bats!
- Ⓑ bats?
- Ⓒ bats

20.
- Ⓕ head?
- Ⓖ head.
- Ⓗ head

GO ON

72   978-1-62057-593-2 *Spectrum Test Practice 1*

Name _____ Date _____

Directions: Look at the sentences as your teacher reads. Choose the sentence that has the correct punctuation and capitalization. Practice with example F. Do the same with numbers 21–26.

Example

F.
- (F) I love winter Time.
- (G) Snowflakes can melt quickly.
- (H) December is a winter month?

21.
- (A) baby cats are Kittens.
- (B) Baby cows are calves.
- (C) A giraffe baby is a calf too

22.
- (F) Jumbo was an elephant.
- (G) children loved Jumbo.
- (H) Have you heard of Him?

23.
- (A) honeybees live in hives.
- (B) They make honey.
- (C) have you ever been stung!

24.
- (F) Apples are a fruit.
- (G) I love Potato Chips!
- (H) celery is crunchy.

25.
- (A) The soccer Ball flew!
- (B) It bounced high!
- (C) the team scored!

26.
- (F) dr. Conrad is nice.
- (G) She checks my teeth.
- (H) she is a dentist!

STOP

LANGUAGE: LANGUAGE EXPRESSION

● **Lesson 9: Usage**

Directions: Listen to your teacher read the sentence and the word choices. Choose the best word to fill in the blank. Practice with examples A and B.

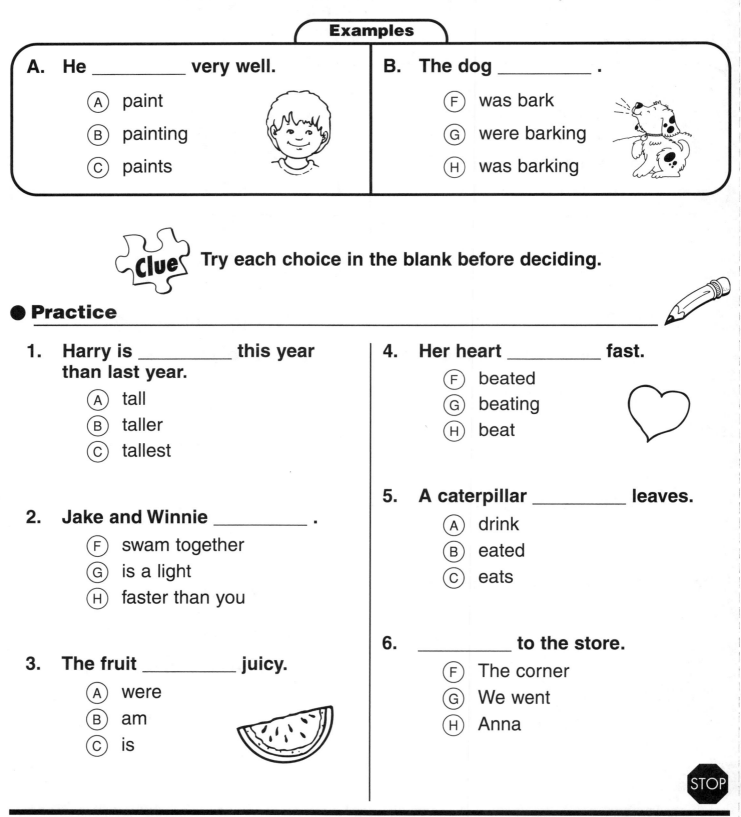

Examples

A. He _____ very well.

   (A) paint

   (B) painting

   (C) paints

B. The dog _____ .

   (F) was bark

   (G) were barking

   (H) was barking

Clue Try each choice in the blank before deciding.

● **Practice**

1. Harry is _____ this year than last year.

   (A) tall

   (B) taller

   (C) tallest

2. Jake and Winnie _____ .

   (F) swam together

   (G) is a light

   (H) faster than you

3. The fruit _____ juicy.

   (A) were

   (B) am

   (C) is

4. Her heart _____ fast.

   (F) beated

   (G) beating

   (H) beat

5. A caterpillar _____ leaves.

   (A) drink

   (B) eated

   (C) eats

6. _____ to the store.

   (F) The corner

   (G) We went

   (H) Anna

STOP

LANGUAGE: LANGUAGE EXPRESSION

● **Lesson 10: Usage**

Directions: Listen to your teacher read the sentence choices. Choose the sentence that is written correctly. Practice with examples A and B.

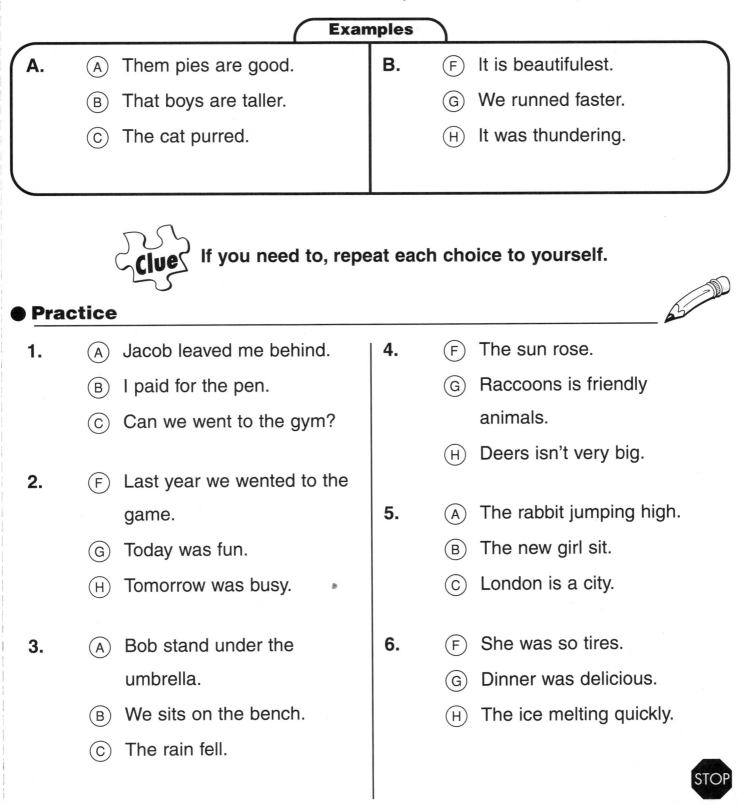

Examples

A.
- Ⓐ Them pies are good.
- Ⓑ That boys are taller.
- Ⓒ The cat purred.

B.
- Ⓕ It is beautifulest.
- Ⓖ We runned faster.
- Ⓗ It was thundering.

Clue If you need to, repeat each choice to yourself.

● **Practice**

1.
- Ⓐ Jacob leaved me behind.
- Ⓑ I paid for the pen.
- Ⓒ Can we went to the gym?

2.
- Ⓕ Last year we wented to the game.
- Ⓖ Today was fun.
- Ⓗ Tomorrow was busy.

3.
- Ⓐ Bob stand under the umbrella.
- Ⓑ We sits on the bench.
- Ⓒ The rain fell.

4.
- Ⓕ The sun rose.
- Ⓖ Raccoons is friendly animals.
- Ⓗ Deers isn't very big.

5.
- Ⓐ The rabbit jumping high.
- Ⓑ The new girl sit.
- Ⓒ London is a city.

6.
- Ⓕ She was so tires.
- Ⓖ Dinner was delicious.
- Ⓗ The ice melting quickly.

STOP

LANGUAGE: LANGUAGE EXPRESSION

● **Lesson 11: Adjectives and Conjunctions**

Directions: Listen to your teacher read each sentence. Choose the word that best fills the blank. Practice with examples A and B.

Examples

A. We could barely see the _____ bugs.

- (A) cold
- (B) tiny
- (C) windy

B. I stayed home _____ I was sick.

- (F) because
- (G) nearby
- (H) or

● **Practice**

1. The river is _____ brown.
   - (A) big
   - (B) hot
   - (C) dark

2. The _____ sand is hot.
   - (F) smart
   - (G) gold
   - (H) funny

3. The _____ children found my toy boat.
   - (A) green
   - (B) little
   - (C) dusty

4. It floated farther ___ farther away.
   - (F) so
   - (G) and
   - (H) because

5. The water was cold, _____ we did not go swimming.
   - (A) because
   - (B) or
   - (C) so

6. Does school start at 7:00 _____ 8:00?
   - (F) and
   - (G) so
   - (H) or

STOP

LANGUAGE: LANGUAGE EXPRESSION

● Lesson 12: Determiners and Prepositions

Directions: Listen to your teacher read each sentence. Choose the word that best fills the blank. Practice with examples A and B.

Examples

A. Decide ____ toy you want to give to the baby.
- (A) that
- (B) which
- (C) those

B. We went ____ the store to the bank.
- (F) about
- (G) over
- (H) from

● Practice

1. How much does _____ toy cost?
   - (A) an
   - (B) what
   - (C) that

2. Where can I find ____ slippers?
   - (F) those
   - (G) that
   - (H) an

3. Look at ___ trees across the road.
   - (A) the
   - (B) what
   - (C) that

4. They should not talk ____ the movie.
   - (F) during
   - (G) toward
   - (H) around

5. Look ____ the road and you will see the barn.
   - (A) beyond
   - (B) about
   - (C) inside

6. Tie the string ____ the balloon.
   - (F) toward
   - (G) around
   - (H) until

STOP

Name _____ Date_____

LANGUAGE: LANGUAGE EXPRESSION

● **Lesson 13: Pronouns**

Directions: Listen to your teacher read the sentences and the word choices. Which pronoun makes sense in place of the underlined part? Mark your choice. Practice with examples A and B.

Examples

A. I saw <u>Jim</u>.
- Ⓐ he
- Ⓑ she
- Ⓒ him

B. We gave <u>the girls</u> candy.
- Ⓕ them
- Ⓖ it
- Ⓗ they

Clue The correct answer means the same as the underlined part.

● **Practice**

1. <u>Opal and I</u> were running.
- Ⓐ Them
- Ⓑ We
- Ⓒ They

2. <u>Jason and Tami</u> are in trouble.
- Ⓕ It
- Ⓖ They
- Ⓗ Us

3. I could not hear <u>my mother</u>.
- Ⓐ her
- Ⓑ she
- Ⓒ them

4. Will you listen to <u>Mrs. Herts</u> when she sings?
- Ⓕ she
- Ⓖ I
- Ⓗ her

5. <u>The sun</u> was very bright.
- Ⓐ His
- Ⓑ It
- Ⓒ Them

6. He is as short as <u>Max</u>.
- Ⓕ he
- Ⓖ they
- Ⓗ him

STOP

━━━━━ LANGUAGE: LANGUAGE EXPRESSION ━━━━━

● **Lesson 14: Sentences**

Directions: Listen to your teacher read the sentences and the answer choices. Think about how the sentence could be turned into a question that makes sense. Choose the best answer. Practice with examples A and B.

Examples

A. **I was early.**
- (A) Early I was?
- (B) Was I early?
- (C) I early was?

B. **The horse is racing.**
- (F) Racing is the horse?
- (G) Is the horse racing?
- (H) Horse racing is the?

Clue Say each answer choice to yourself.

● **Practice**

1. **Bert was in the play.**
- (A) In the play was Bert?
- (B) Was the play in Bert?
- (C) Was Bert in the play?

3. **My name is Conrad.**
- (A) Conrad my name is?
- (B) Is Conrad my name?
- (C) Name my Conrad is?

2. **They will go skating.**
- (F) Will they go skating?
- (G) Go skating will they?
- (H) Skating will they go?

4. **The flower was in bloom.**
- (F) Was the flower in bloom?
- (G) In bloom was the flower?
- (H) The flower in bloom was?

STOP

LANGUAGE: LANGUAGE EXPRESSION

● **Lesson 15: Sentences**

Directions: Listen to your teacher read these groups of words. Choose which group is a complete sentence. Practice with examples A and B.

Examples

A.
- Ⓐ To the store.
- Ⓑ The tree is tall.
- Ⓒ Won the race.

B.
- Ⓕ The butterfly.
- Ⓖ Sun rose.
- Ⓗ The moon is full.

 **Clue** Say each answer choice to yourself.

● **Practice**

1.
- Ⓐ Our yard.
- Ⓑ It rained all night.
- Ⓒ Jumped up.

2.
- Ⓕ Chip flew the kite high.
- Ⓖ Under the rock.
- Ⓗ Some people.

3.
- Ⓐ Phone number is.
- Ⓑ Bird nests.
- Ⓒ Paco has a new coat.

4.
- Ⓕ When was the?
- Ⓖ Was open all day.
- Ⓗ He picked the biggest one.

5.
- Ⓐ Read the.
- Ⓑ To the zoo.
- Ⓒ It snows in the winter.

6.
- Ⓕ Babies like rattles.
- Ⓖ Likes to sing.
- Ⓗ Fish and frogs.

LANGUAGE: LANGUAGE EXPRESSION

● **Lesson 16: Paragraphs**

Directions: A paragraph is a group of sentences all about the same idea. Listen to your teacher read the groups of sentences and the answer choices. Choose the sentence that best completes the paragraph. Practice together with example A.

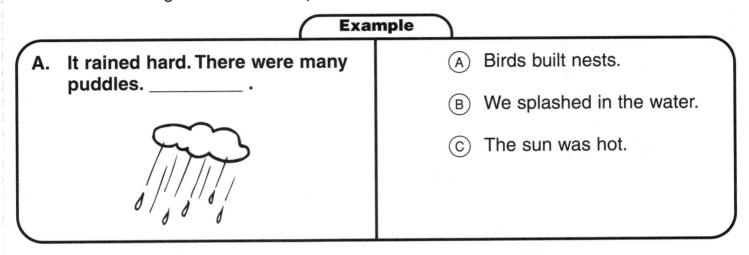

Example

A.   **It rained hard. There were many puddles. _____ .**

Ⓐ Birds built nests.

Ⓑ We splashed in the water.

Ⓒ The sun was hot.

 **Clue** The correct answer fits best with the other sentences.

● **Practice**

1.   **Hanna sat down to read. She read a long time. _____ .**

Ⓐ She finished the book.

Ⓑ It was her brother's dog.

Ⓒ The radio was loud.

2.   **The family went on a trip. They were going far away. _____ .**

Ⓕ They went on skates.

Ⓖ They took an airplane.

Ⓗ Kim did not like the apple.

3.   **It was so dark. I looked up at the sky. _____ .**

Ⓐ I ate a cookie.

Ⓑ I saw many stars.

Ⓒ The grass was cool.

4.   **Vera is my sister. She is older than me. _____ .**

Ⓕ My dog is black.

Ⓖ She is also taller than me.

Ⓗ Our cat purrs.

STOP

LANGUAGE: LANGUAGE EXPRESSION
SAMPLE TEST

Directions: Listen to your teacher read the sentences and choose the word that best fills in the blank. Practice with example A.

Directions: Listen to your teacher read the sentences and choose the sentence that is written correctly. Practice with example B.

Examples

A. Betty _____ lots of books.
- (A) reads
- (B) readed
- (C) reading

B.
- (F) I lives by Kim.
- (G) Peter running to the corner.
- (H) It is very hot.

---

1. The _____ scored three points.
- (A) team
- (B) ball
- (C) net

2. _____ were jumping rope.
- (F) The trees
- (G) Four girls
- (H) Mrs. Connor

3. The _____ tasted great!
- (A) car
- (B) boat
- (C) cake

4.
- (F) They raking leaves.
- (G) I loves her very much.
- (H) We went to Tokyo.

5.
- (A) Will Grandfather comes too?
- (B) Uncle Torres is old.
- (C) Mine hair is gray.

6.
- (F) The pictures is ripped.
- (G) We are freezing!
- (H) The apple fallen.

GO ON

LANGUAGE: LANGUAGE EXPRESSION
SAMPLE TEST (cont.)

Directions: Listen to your teacher read the sentences. As your teacher reads, look at the underlined part. Choose the pronoun that best replaces it. Practice with example C.

Directions: Listen to your teacher read the sentences. As you listen to your teacher, think about how the sentence sounds best as a question. Practice with example D.

Examples

C. **<u>The plant</u> was green.**
- Ⓐ They
- Ⓑ It
- Ⓒ Them

D. **My hair is long.**
- Ⓕ Hair long is my?
- Ⓖ Is my hair long?
- Ⓗ Long is my hair?

7. **Tina bought <u>my mother</u> some candy.**
- Ⓐ she
- Ⓑ them
- Ⓒ her

8. **<u>Lonny and I</u> are leaving.**
- Ⓕ We
- Ⓖ Him
- Ⓗ It

9. **May I help <u>Mike</u> do that?**
- Ⓐ he
- Ⓑ I
- Ⓒ him

10. **This is a fun project.**
- Ⓕ Is this a fun project?
- Ⓖ A fun project this is?
- Ⓗ A project fun this is?

11. **Kate's kite was stuck.**
- Ⓐ Stuck was Kate's kite?
- Ⓑ Was Kate's kite stuck?
- Ⓒ Was stuck Kate's kite?

12. **My soda is gone.**
- Ⓕ My soda gone is?
- Ⓖ Gone is my soda?
- Ⓗ Is my soda gone?

GO ON

Name _____ Date _____

LANGUAGE: LANGUAGE EXPRESSION
SAMPLE TEST (cont.)

Directions: Listen to your teacher read the sentences and choose the answer that is a complete sentence for numbers 13–15. Practice with example E.

Directions: Listen to your teacher read the sentences and choose the best sentence to complete the paragraph for numbers 16–18. Practice with example F.

Examples

E.
- (A) The tree lost its leaves.
- (B) In the closet.
- (C) A huge box.

F. **Allie was crying. She had fallen.** _____ .
- (F) She hurt her knee.
- (G) She ate cake.
- (H) It was yellow.

13.
- (A) Cutting the paper.
- (B) In the shed.
- (C) We all ate oranges.

14.
- (F) Yesterday.
- (G) Today was sunny.
- (H) Live in our barn.

15.
- (A) Tommy washes the car.
- (B) Cleaned the stove.
- (C) Did the laundry.

16. **Grant and Ellie went fishing. Ellie had a bite!** _____ .
- (F) Grant drank milk.
- (G) She caught a fish.
- (H) Birds fly south.

17. **We do chores. I do the dishes.** _____ .
- (A) The dog barks.
- (B) My dad likes coffee.
- (C) My brother puts the dishes away.

18. **Dad was making popcorn. He burned it!** _____ .
- (F) Mom opened a window.
- (G) Sparky ran in circles.
- (H) Can we go now?

978-1-62057-593-2 *Spectrum Test Practice 1*

LANGUAGE: SPELLING

● **Lesson 17: Spelling Skills**

Directions: Look at each word carefully. Which word is spelled **correctly**? Choose the best answer. Practice with examples A and B.

Examples

A.
- (A) car
- (B) cahr
- (C) carr

B.
- (F) bote
- (G) boat
- (H) boate

Clue If you are not sure which answer is correct, take your best guess. Eliminate answer choices you know are wrong.

● **Practice**

1.
- (A) darc
- (B) dahrk
- (C) dark

2.
- (F) furst
- (G) first
- (H) ferst

3.
- (A) summer
- (B) sumer
- (C) sammer

4.
- (F) perty
- (G) pretty
- (H) pretey

5.
- (A) depe
- (B) deep
- (C) deap

6.
- (F) papper
- (G) paiper
- (H) paper

STOP

LANGUAGE: SPELLING

● **Lesson 18: Spelling Skills**

Directions: Look at each group of words. Which word in each group is **not** spelled correctly? Practice with examples A and B.

Examples

A.
- (A) shell
- (B) smile
- (C) laike

B.
- (F) frunt
- (G) pin
- (H) game

Clue If you are not sure which answer is correct, take your best guess.

● **Practice**

1.
- (A) brown
- (B) grean
- (C) white

2.
- (F) therd
- (G) second
- (H) first

3.
- (A) park
- (B) bank
- (C) trunck

4.
- (F) buzz
- (G) showd
- (H) talk

5.
- (A) kite
- (B) playng
- (C) balloon

6.
- (F) mahl
- (G) school
- (H) store

STOP

LANGUAGE: SPELLING
SAMPLE TEST

Directions: Look at each word carefully. Which word is spelled correctly? Choose the best answer. Practice with examples A and B. Do numbers 1–6 the same way.

Examples

A.
- (A) whin
- (B) win
- (C) wen

B.
- (F) there
- (G) thair
- (H) thare

1.
- (A) somethin
- (B) sumthing
- (C) something

2.
- (F) right
- (G) ryte
- (H) riht

3.
- (A) nekst
- (B) next
- (C) nxt

4.
- (F) fownd
- (G) foun
- (H) found

5.
- (A) teach
- (B) teech
- (C) teich

6.
- (F) girl
- (G) gurl
- (H) grrl

GO ON

LANGUAGE: SPELLING
SAMPLE TEST (cont.)

Directions: Look at the groups of words. Which word in each group is **not** spelled correctly? Practice with examples C and D. Do numbers 7–12 the same way.

Examples

C.
- (A) dri
- (B) pill
- (C) feel

D.
- (F) which
- (G) list
- (H) sutch

7.
- (A) toek
- (B) while
- (C) mother

8.
- (F) ten
- (G) tell
- (H) truble

9.
- (A) stop
- (B) gote
- (C) went

10.
- (F) again
- (G) that's
- (H) blak

11.
- (A) much
- (B) stood
- (C) ahr

12.
- (F) thenk
- (G) my
- (H) near

STOP

LANGUAGE: STUDY SKILLS

● **Lesson 19: Study Skills**

Directions: Look at the words as your teacher reads them. Choose the word that comes first in ABC order. Practice with example A.

Directions: Listen to your teacher read the sentences and the answer choices. Mark the best answer. Practice with example B.

Examples

A.	Which word comes first in ABC order?
	(A) queen
	(B) bowl
	(C) pin

B.	If you need the meaning of a word, you look in a _____ .
	(F) map
	(G) dictionary
	(H) pencil

Clue Stay with your first answer choice.

● **Practice**

1. (A) flew
    (B) zip
    (C) hill

2. (F) just
    (G) time
    (H) door

3. (A) head
    (B) yawn
    (C) line

4. **Steve needs directions to a city. Where might he look?**

    (F) a map
    (G) a dictionary
    (H) a bottle

5. **My report is about cooking. I talked to a _____ about it.**

    (A) police officer
    (B) chef
    (C) doctor

STOP

89

LANGUAGE: STUDY SKILLS

● **Lesson 20: Study Skills**

Directions: Read the table of contents with your teacher. It tells the names of chapters and what pages they are on in the book. Use it to answer the questions your teacher reads. Practice with example A.

Example

Table of Contents
Chapter 1—Rivers 3
Chapter 2—Lakes 6
Chapter 3—Seas 9
Chapter 4—Oceans 13

A. **On which page will Maggie find information on oceans?**

Ⓐ 6
Ⓑ 3
Ⓒ 13

Clue Look at the table of contents with your teacher before starting the questions.

● **Practice**

Shelly wrote a report. It is about animals in the zoo. Here is her table of contents. Use it to answer the questions.

Table of Contents
Chapter 1—
Reptile House 2
Chapter 2—
Aquarium .4
Chapter 3—
Animals from North America 8
Chapter 4—
Animals from Africa 10

1. **Which chapter tells about fish?**

Ⓐ 2
Ⓑ 4
Ⓒ 3

2. **How many chapters are about animals from Africa?**

Ⓕ 4
Ⓖ 1
Ⓗ 10

3. **What is another chapter Shelly could include?**

Ⓐ Cars and Trucks
Ⓑ My Dog
Ⓒ Animals from South America

STOP

LANGUAGE: STUDY SKILLS
SAMPLE TEST

Directions: Listen to your teacher read the sentences and answer choices. Choose the best answer. Practice with examples A and B.

Examples

A. Which word comes first in ABC order?

- (A) keep
- (B) leap
- (C) bird

B. A table of contents shows _____ .

- (F) chapter names and pages
- (G) problems
- (H) definitions

For numbers 1–3, choose the word that comes first in ABC order.

1.
- (A) front
- (B) water
- (C) apple

2.
- (F) come
- (G) show
- (H) meet

3.
- (A) follow
- (B) three
- (C) bell

Will wrote a report about his grandfather's store. Use the table of contents at the top of the next column to help you answer questions 4 and 5.

Table of Contents

Chapter 1—
Opening the Shoe Store 2
Chapter 2—
What Kinds of Shoes 4
Chapter 3—
How to Make a Shoe 8
Chapter 4—
Selling Shoes 10

4. What page has information on making a shoe?
- (F) 8
- (G) 7
- (H) 1

5. Which chapter number tells about the types of shoes grandfather sells?
- (A) 1
- (B) 2
- (C) 3

STOP

Name _____ Date_____

● **Lesson 21: Writing**

Directions: On a separate sheet of paper, write a response to each prompt. Include all the parts in the checklists.

1. **Write an Opinion**
   Write about your favorite animal. Tell why it is your favorite. Tell why someone else should like it, too.

Checklist:

Read what you wrote. Did you remember to do the following?

	Yes	No
Introduce the topic.	☐	☐
State what you think.	☐	☐
Give a good reason for what you think.	☐	☐
Write a good ending.	☐	☐

2. **Write an Opinion**
   Write about your favorite book. Tell what part you like best. Tell why someone else should read the book.

Checklist:

Read what you wrote. Did you remember to do the following?

	Yes	No
Introduce the topic.	☐	☐
State what you think.	☐	☐
Give a good reason for what you think.	☐	☐
Write a good ending.	☐	☐

3. **Write to Inform**
   Write about your family. Give information about each family member.

Checklist:

Read what you wrote. Did you remember to do the following?

	Yes	No
Introduce the topic.	☐	☐
Give facts about your topic.	☐	☐
Write an ending that makes sense.	☐	☐

GO ON →

Name _____ Date _____

● **Lesson 21: Writing (cont.)**

4. **Write to Inform**

Write about your neighborhood. Explain who lives in your neighborhood. Describe buildings in your neighborhood.

Checklist:

Read what you wrote. Did you remember to do the following?

	Yes	**No**
Introduce the topic.	☐	☐
Give facts about your topic.	☐	☐
Write an ending that makes sense.	☐	☐

5. **Write a Narrative**

Write about a time you were really happy. Tell what happened in order.

Checklist:

Read what you wrote. Did you remember to do the following?

	Yes	**No**
Include important events in order.	☐	☐
Use details to help the reader understand.	☐	☐
Use words like **next** or **then** to explain the order of events.	☐	☐
Write an ending that makes sense.	☐	☐

6. **Write a Narrative**

Write a story about a talking dog who gets into trouble. Tell what happens in order.

Checklist:

Read what you wrote. Did you remember to do the following?

	Yes	**No**
Include important events in order.	☐	☐
Use details to help the reader understand.	☐	☐
Use words like **next** or **then** to explain the order of events.	☐	☐
Write an ending that makes sense.	☐	☐

LANGUAGE PRACTICE TEST

● **Part 1: Listening**

Directions: Listen to your teacher read the story. Choose the best answer for each question. Practice with example A. Do the same for numbers 1–7.

Example

A. Teri knows how to make a sandwich. She can show us how. First, you need bread. Then you put it in the toaster. What is next?

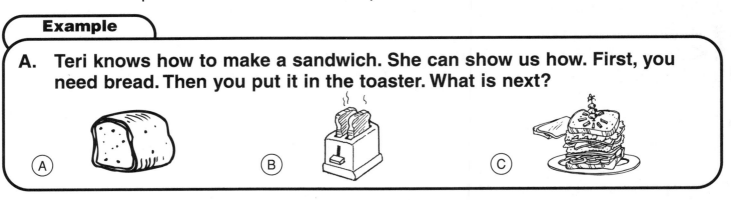

Ⓐ   Ⓑ   Ⓒ

1. There are many sounds. Sounds come from many things. Some are very loud. Others are very quiet. Which would make a very quiet sound?

Ⓐ   Ⓑ   Ⓒ

2. Vince wrote a report. It was about animals. Some animals are big. Other animals are small. He drew two pictures. One had big animals on it and one had small animals. Which animal would go on the picture of big animals?

Ⓕ   Ⓖ   Ⓗ

3. Maisie planted many seeds. She had a big garden. Later, Maisie picked good things to eat. Which picture shows something Maisie might leave in the garden?

Ⓐ   Ⓑ   Ⓒ   GO ON ⇨

LANGUAGE PRACTICE TEST
Part 1: Listening (cont.)

4. The class worked very hard. They read many books. The prize is a pizza party. Mrs. Smith is going to buy the pizzas. The party is tomorrow. How do the students feel?

Ⓕ   Ⓖ   Ⓗ

5. Teddy looked up. He saw something in the sky. It was full of color. He wanted to catch it! He watched as it flew up. What did Teddy see?

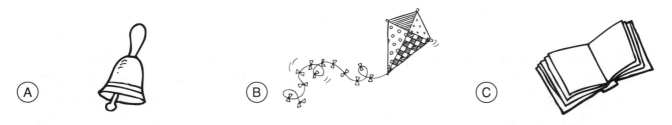

Ⓐ   Ⓑ   Ⓒ

6. After dinner we had a treat. The treat was sweet. It was cool. We had to eat fast or it might melt. What was for dessert?

Ⓕ   Ⓖ   Ⓗ

7. Jessie had homework. She sat down in her room. She had everything she needed. Now she would start working. What won't she use to do her homework?

Ⓐ   Ⓑ   Ⓒ

GO ON

LANGUAGE PRACTICE TEST

● **Part 1: Listening (cont.)**

Directions: Listen to your teacher read the story and answer choices. Choose the best answer to the question. Practice with example B. Do the same for numbers 8–10.

Example

B. Many people eat pizza. It can have many things on top. Some good things are cheese and meat. Some people like pizza with vegetables. Some even like it with fruit! Pizza needs to bake. Where would you bake a pizza?

(F) an oven
(G) a car
(H) a library

8. My family went to the beach. It was very hot. The sky was blue. We wore shorts. We collected shells. Mother brought lunch. We ate on the sand. Where did the family go?

(F) sky
(G) beach
(H) store

9. Jack saved his money. He had a bank. It was so heavy! He had a plan. He wanted a bike. It was blue and black. He knew it would go fast. What did Jack want to buy?

(A) a bank
(B) a blue shirt
(C) a bike

10. Mina had ten stickers. She wanted to share. She gave three to her brother. She gave three to her sister. Mother said she was a good girl. Mina gave her mother a sticker too! How many stickers did Mina give to her Mother?

(F) 1
(G) 3
(H) 0

STOP

LANGUAGE PRACTICE TEST

● **Part 2: Language Mechanics**

Directions: Listen to your teacher read each sentence. Which word in the sentence needs to be capitalized? If no more capital letters are needed, choose None. Practice with examples A and B. Do the same for 1–4.

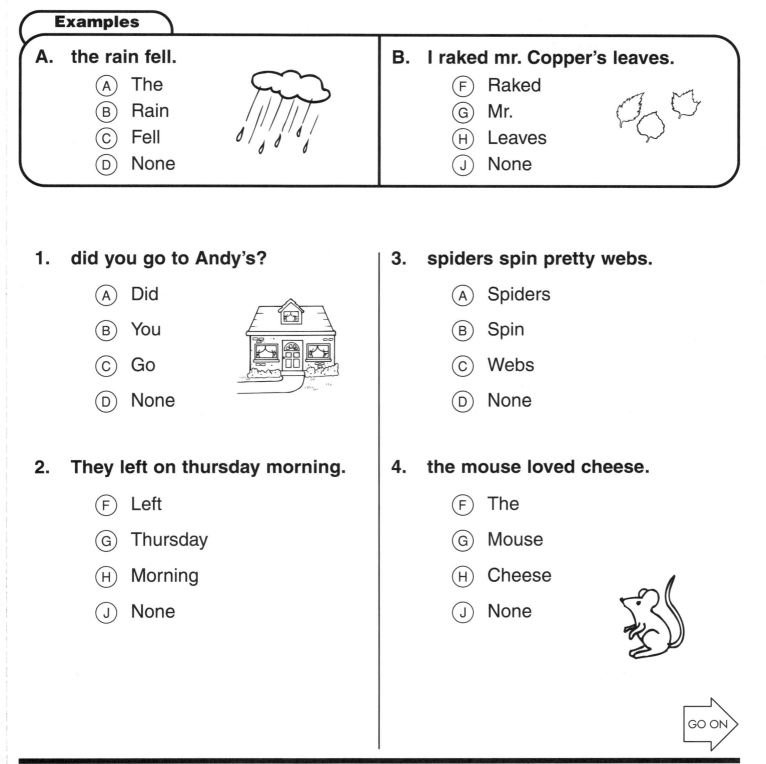

Examples

A.   the rain fell.

    Ⓐ The

    Ⓑ Rain

    Ⓒ Fell

    Ⓓ None

B.   I raked mr. Copper's leaves.

    Ⓕ Raked

    Ⓖ Mr.

    Ⓗ Leaves

    Ⓙ None

1.   did you go to Andy's?

    Ⓐ Did

    Ⓑ You

    Ⓒ Go

    Ⓓ None

2.   They left on thursday morning.

    Ⓕ Left

    Ⓖ Thursday

    Ⓗ Morning

    Ⓙ None

3.   spiders spin pretty webs.

    Ⓐ Spiders

    Ⓑ Spin

    Ⓒ Webs

    Ⓓ None

4.   the mouse loved cheese.

    Ⓕ The

    Ⓖ Mouse

    Ⓗ Cheese

    Ⓙ None

GO ON

Name _____ Date _____

LANGUAGE PRACTICE TEST

● **Part 2: Language Mechanics (cont.)**

Directions: Listen to your teacher read each story. Look at the underlined part. Think about how it should be written. Choose the best answer. Practice with example C. Do numbers 5–8 the same way.

Example

C. The trip was long. We were going to <u>aunt sue's</u> house.	(A) Aunt sue's (B) Aunt Sue's (C) The way it is.

Playing Soccer

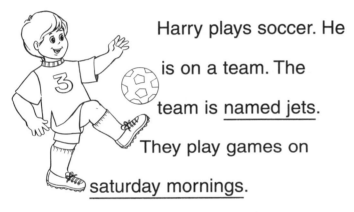

Harry plays soccer. He is on a team. The team is <u>named jets</u>. They play games on <u>saturday mornings</u>.

5. **Look at the first underlined part. How should it be written?**

   (A) named Jets
   (B) Named Jets
   (C) The way it is.

6. **Look at the second underlined part. How should it be written?**

   (F) satur Day mornings
   (G) Saturday mornings
   (H) The way it is.

School News

The first day of school is fun. We meet new teachers. We make new friends. My new teacher is tall. His name is <u>Mr. fuller</u>. He is <u>from Spain</u>.

7. **Look at the first underlined part. How should it be written?**

   (A) Mr. Fuller
   (B) mr. fuller
   (C) The way it is.

8. **Look at the second underlined part. How should it be written?**

   (F) From Spain
   (G) from spain
   (H) The way it is.

GO ON

═══ LANGUAGE PRACTICE TEST ═══

● **Part 2: Language Mechanics (cont.)**

Directions: Listen to your teacher read the sentences. Some may need punctuation at the end. Choose the correct punctuation mark. If none is needed, mark None. Practice with examples D and E. Do the same for 9–14.

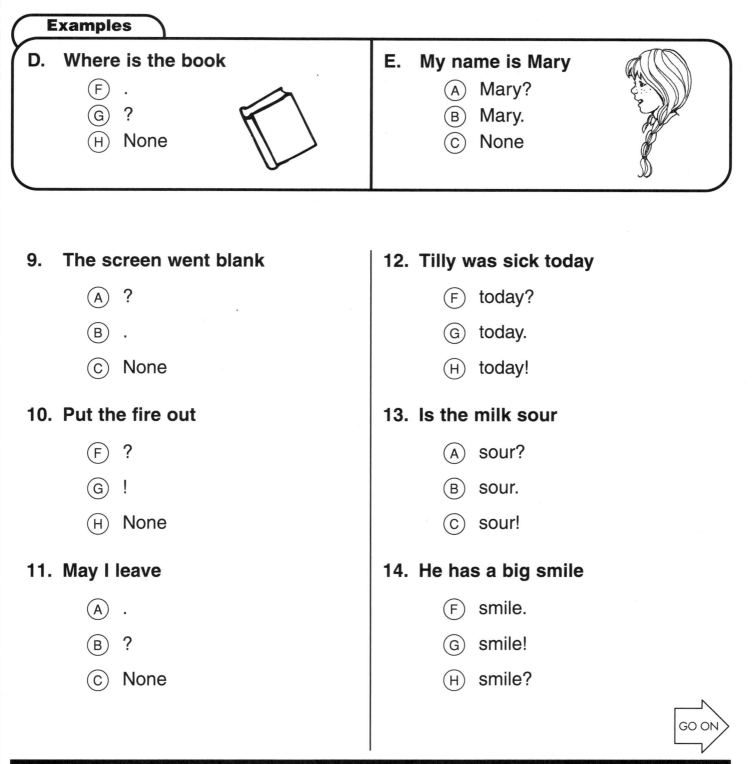

Examples

D.   Where is the book
- (F)   .
- (G)   ?
- (H)   None

E.   My name is Mary
- (A)   Mary?
- (B)   Mary.
- (C)   None

9.   **The screen went blank**
- (A)   ?
- (B)   .
- (C)   None

10.   **Put the fire out**
- (F)   ?
- (G)   !
- (H)   None

11.   **May I leave**
- (A)   .
- (B)   ?
- (C)   None

12.   **Tilly was sick today**
- (F)   today?
- (G)   today.
- (H)   today!

13.   **Is the milk sour**
- (A)   sour?
- (B)   sour.
- (C)   sour!

14.   **He has a big smile**
- (F)   smile.
- (G)   smile!
- (H)   smile?

GO ON

LANGUAGE PRACTICE TEST

● **Part 2: Language Mechanics (cont.)**

Directions: Listen to your teacher read each sentence. Look at the words. Do they need capital letters or punctuation? Choose the sentence that is written correctly. Practice with examples F and G. Do the same with numbers 15–20.

Examples

F.		
	(F)	my hands are blue
	(G)	I am cold.
	(H)	i have a cold.

G.		
	(A)	Sara ran backwards.
	(B)	the dog was sleeping
	(C)	tim jumps high!

---

15. (A) I have a red pen
     (B) kurt has black hair.
     (C) Nina dropped the spoon.

16. (F) The paint is dry.
     (G) cora is ten.
     (H) Sela cannot Come?

17. (A) Peggy was quiet
     (B) he wrote the letter.
     (C) Zack heard crying.

18. (F) Jamal Won the Contest.
     (G) Blueberries are my favorite
     (H) Should we leave?

19. (A) I will see you
     (B) can dennis type
     (C) He is so tall!

20. (F) Give me a hug.
     (G) the soup tastes good?
     (H) I am Finished.

STOP

LANGUAGE PRACTICE TEST

● **Part 3: Language Expression**

Directions: Listen to your teacher read the sentences and answer choices. Choose the word that best completes the sentence. Practice with example A.

Directions: Listen to your teacher read the answer choices. Choose the words that make up a sentence that is correctly written. Practice with example B.

Examples

A. **Aunt Stella _____ good soup.**
- (A) cooking
- (B) cook
- (C) cooks

B.
- (F) Now the group.
- (G) The middle part.
- (H) I ate the muffin.

1. **The _____ was deep.**
- (A) rivers
- (B) river
- (C) rivering

2. **Bess _____ horses well.**
- (F) drawing
- (G) draws
- (H) drawed

3. **The shelf _____ .**
- (A) falling
- (B) falled
- (C) fell

4.
- (F) Push the.
- (G) Harvey rode the train.
- (H) Cart fast.

5.
- (A) Buddy was a.
- (B) Big raindrops.
- (C) It is cloudy.

6.
- (F) Saturday will be fun!
- (G) The picnic.
- (H) Next week won't never be busy.

GO ON

LANGUAGE PRACTICE TEST

● **Part 3: Language Expression (cont.)**

Directions: Listen to your teacher read the sentences and answer choices. Choose the best pronoun to replace the underlined words. Practice with example C.

Directions: Listen to your teacher read the sentences and answer choices. Choose the sentence that should come next. Practice with example D.

Examples

C. **We went to see <u>Petra and Bill</u>.**
- (A) they
- (B) them
- (C) him

D. **The dish broke. There was a mess. _____ .**
- (F) Mom was upset.
- (G) Jimmy was sleeping.
- (H) It is my birthday.

7. **<u>Marion</u> had chicken pox.**
- (A) Her
- (B) She
- (C) They

8. **<u>Hilda and I</u> were right!**
- (F) We
- (G) Us
- (H) Them

9. **<u>My bike and skates</u> are broken.**
- (A) They
- (B) Its
- (C) I

10. **Some food comes from animals. Milk comes from cows.**
_____ .
- (F) Eggs come from chickens.
- (G) Pumpkins grow fast.
- (H) Pigs like mud.

11. **Skunks are small mammals. They are black and white. They can give off a bad smell. Some skunks live in holes. _____ .**
- (A) Birds fly high.
- (B) Skunks eat bugs, mice, and eggs.
- (C) The snake was long.

STOP

LANGUAGE PRACTICE TEST

● Part 4: Spelling

Directions: Look at the groups of words. Choose the word that is spelled **correctly**. Practice with examples A and B.

Examples

A.		B.	
Ⓐ jump		Ⓕ feal	
Ⓑ jamp		Ⓖ feil	
Ⓒ jhumpx		Ⓗ feel	

1.
Ⓐ parte
Ⓑ pahty
Ⓒ party

2.
Ⓕ some
Ⓖ sume
Ⓗ soom

3.
Ⓐ graet
Ⓑ grat
Ⓒ great

4.
Ⓕ hurrt
Ⓖ hurt
Ⓗ hert

5.
Ⓐ whar
Ⓑ wair
Ⓒ where

6.
Ⓕ wish
Ⓖ wesh
Ⓗ wich

GO ON

LANGUAGE PRACTICE TEST

● **Part 4: Spelling (cont.)**

Directions: Look at the groups of words. Choose the word that is **not** spelled correctly. Practice with examples C and D.

Examples

C.
- (A) will
- (B) them
- (C) triy

D.
- (F) stand
- (G) hant
- (H) pin

7.
- (A) way
- (B) night
- (C) thu

10.
- (F) both
- (G) werm
- (H) very

8.
- (F) wuz
- (G) nine
- (H) stop

11.
- (A) pack
- (B) liddle
- (C) pass

9.
- (A) for
- (B) fill
- (C) sed

12.
- (F) all
- (G) eye
- (H) unter

STOP

LANGUAGE PRACTICE TEST

● **Part 5: Study Skills**

Directions: Listen to your teacher read the story. Choose the best answer for each question. Practice with example A.

Example

Sonya Lee will write about puppies. She will write about how to care for them.

A. Who should Sonya Lee talk to about puppies?

Ⓐ a veterinarian

Ⓑ a mailman

Ⓒ a painter

Marnie wrote a story. It was about a trip. She went to a farm. The farm had many animals. She petted the rabbits. She milked a cow. She helped feed the pigs. The farmer showed her the field. It had corn growing in it. Marnie picked an ear of corn.

Here is Marnie's table of contents.

Table of Contents

1. **Marnie will put the animals in her report in ABC order. Which animal comes first?**

   Ⓐ rabbit

   Ⓑ cow

   Ⓒ pig

3. **In which chapter will Marnie put the animals in ABC order?**

   Ⓐ 1

   Ⓑ 2

   Ⓒ 4

2. **Who did Marnie talk to about the farm?**

   Ⓕ her teacher

   Ⓖ farmer

   Ⓗ Mr. Vera

4. **On what page does she talk about the surprise she saw on the farm?**

   Ⓕ 2

   Ⓖ 4

   Ⓗ 10

STOP

MATH: CONCEPTS

● **Lesson 1: Numeration**

Directions: Look at the pictures. Listen to your teacher read the question. Choose the best answer. Practice with example A.

Example

A. **Which bear is the biggest?**

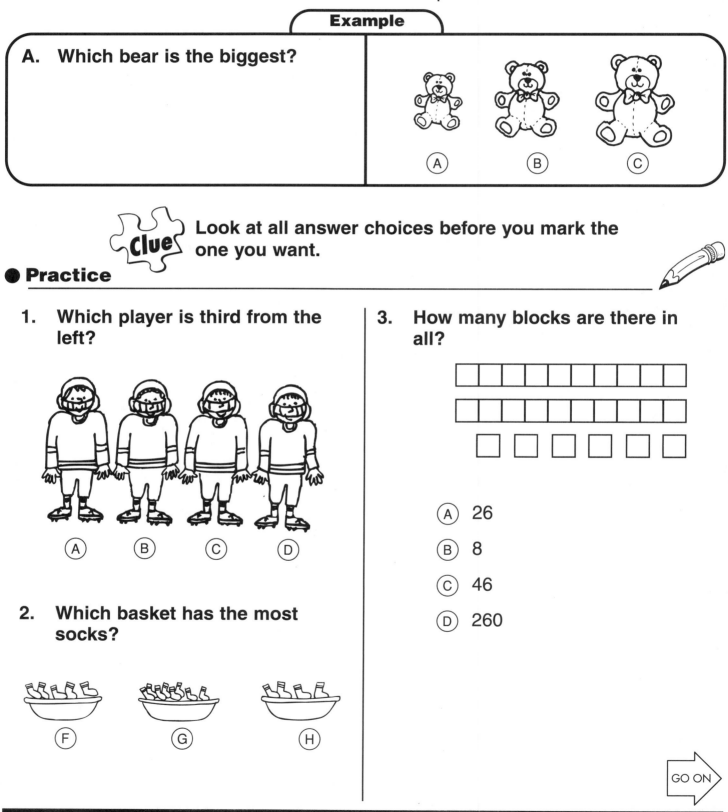

Ⓐ   Ⓑ   Ⓒ

Clue Look at all answer choices before you mark the one you want.

● **Practice**

1. **Which player is third from the left?**

Ⓐ   Ⓑ   Ⓒ   Ⓓ

2. **Which basket has the most socks?**

Ⓕ   Ⓖ   Ⓗ

3. **How many blocks are there in all?**

Ⓐ 26

Ⓑ 8

Ⓒ 46

Ⓓ 260

GO ON

MATH: CONCEPTS

● **Lesson 1: Numeration (cont.)**

4. **How many blocks are there in all?**

- F two
- G seven
- H three
- J eleven

5. **Which picture shows the carrot above the rabbit?**

- A
- B
- C

6. **Which number shows 4 tens and 5 ones?**

- F 405
- G 45
- H 9
- J 54

7. **Which number shows 10 tens and 2 ones?**

- A 10
- B 102
- C 120
- D 201

STOP

MATH: CONCEPTS

● **Lesson 2: Sequencing**

Directions: Look at the pictures. Listen to your teacher read the question. Choose the best answer. Practice with example A.

Example

A. How many candles are on the cake?

- (A) 7
- (B) 6
- (C) 9

Clue If you are not sure which answer is correct, take your best guess.

● **Practice**

1. Which picture shows the bears smallest to largest?

   (A)

   (B)

   (C)

2. Count by ones. Which number comes after 15?

   - (F) 14
   - (G) 25
   - (H) 16
   - (J) 10

3. Which pattern needs the number 8 in the blank?

   - (A) 0, 1, 2, ____
   - (B) 2, 4, 6, ____
   - (C) 18, 28, 38, ____
   - (D) 3, 6, 9, ____

GO ON

MATH: CONCEPTS

● **Lesson 2: Sequencing (cont.)**

4. **What is missing from this pattern?**

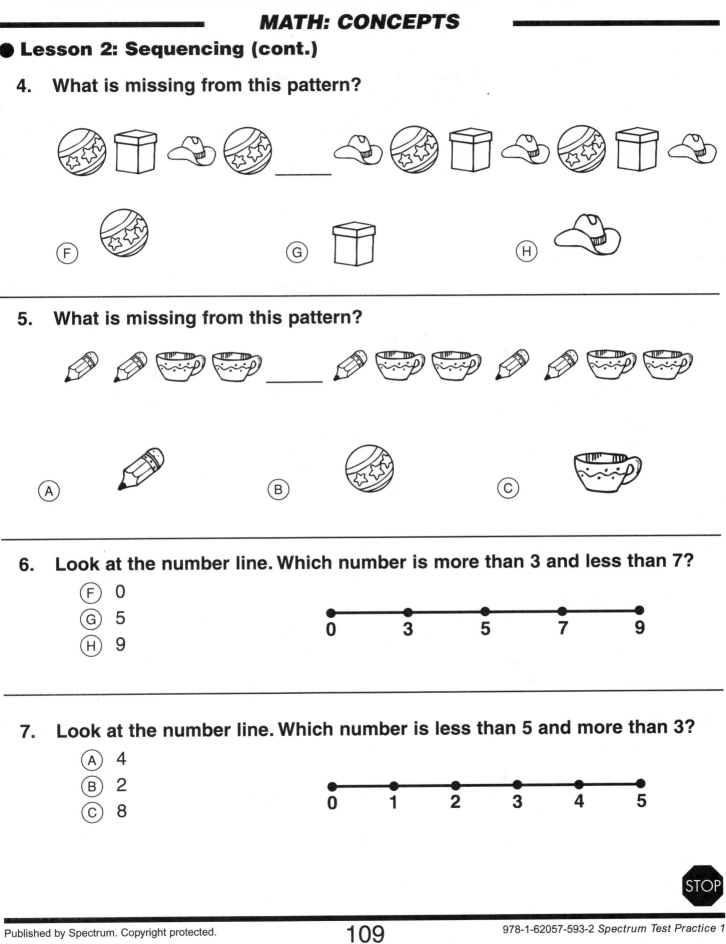

5. **What is missing from this pattern?**

6. **Look at the number line. Which number is more than 3 and less than 7?**
    - (F) 0
    - (G) 5
    - (H) 9

7. **Look at the number line. Which number is less than 5 and more than 3?**
    - (A) 4
    - (B) 2
    - (C) 8

Name _____   Date _____

MATH: CONCEPTS

● Lesson 3: Number Concepts

Directions: Look at the pictures and numbers. Listen to your teacher read the question. Choose the best answer. Practice with example A.

Example

A. Which number shows eleven?

Ⓐ 12
Ⓑ 11
Ⓒ 110
Ⓓ 111

Clue Be sure the space you mark is for the answer you think is correct.

● Practice

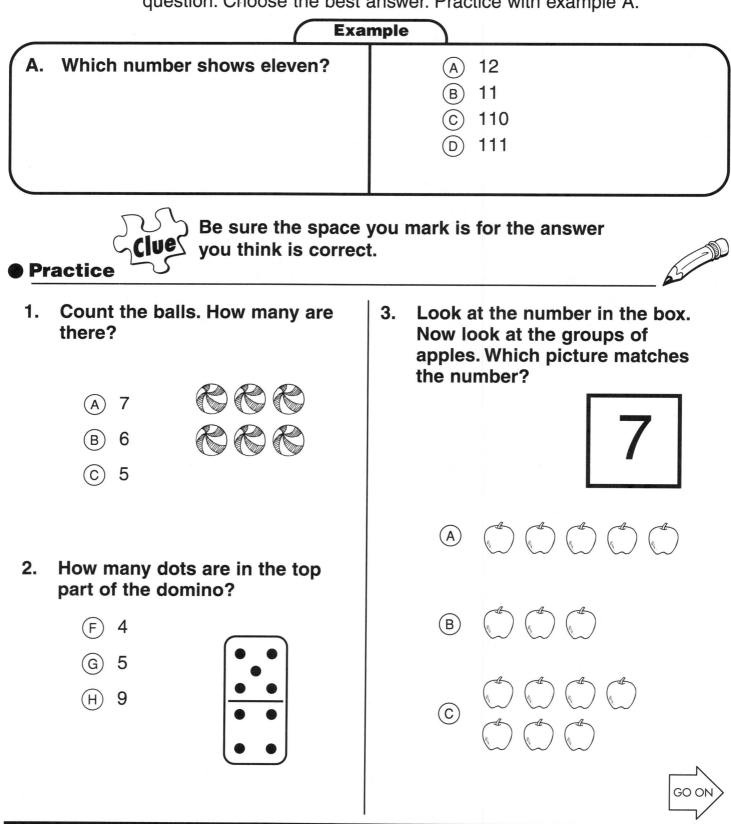

1. **Count the balls. How many are there?**

Ⓐ 7
Ⓑ 6
Ⓒ 5

2. **How many dots are in the top part of the domino?**

Ⓕ 4
Ⓖ 5
Ⓗ 9

3. **Look at the number in the box. Now look at the groups of apples. Which picture matches the number?**

7

Ⓐ

Ⓑ

Ⓒ

GO ON

978-1-62057-593-2 *Spectrum Test Practice 1*

MATH: CONCEPTS

● Lesson 3: Number Concepts (cont.)

4. **Which number is the same as the word in the box?**

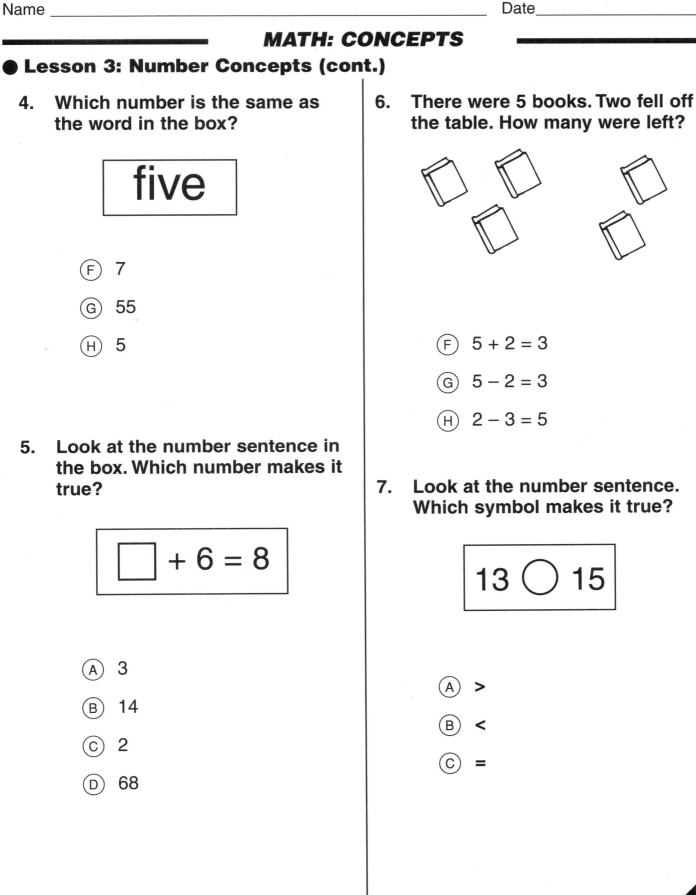

five

- (F) 7
- (G) 55
- (H) 5

5. **Look at the number sentence in the box. Which number makes it true?**

$$\square + 6 = 8$$

- (A) 3
- (B) 14
- (C) 2
- (D) 68

6. **There were 5 books. Two fell off the table. How many were left?**

- (F) $5 + 2 = 3$
- (G) $5 - 2 = 3$
- (H) $2 - 3 = 5$

7. **Look at the number sentence. Which symbol makes it true?**

$$13 \bigcirc 15$$

- (A) >
- (B) <
- (C) =

STOP

MATH: CONCEPTS

● Lesson 4: Patterns and Place Values

Directions: Look at the pictures. Listen to your teacher read the question. Choose the best answer for the question. Practice with example A.

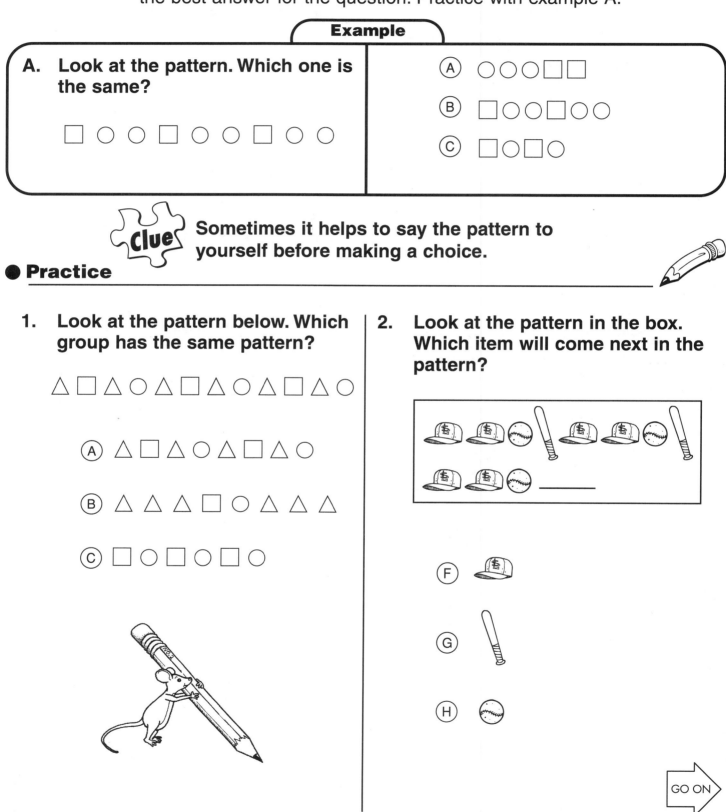

Example

A. Look at the pattern. Which one is the same?

☐ ○ ○ ○ ☐ ○ ○ ☐ ○ ○

Ⓐ ○ ○ ○ ☐ ☐

Ⓑ ☐ ○ ○ ☐ ○ ○

Ⓒ ☐ ○ ☐ ○

Clue Sometimes it helps to say the pattern to yourself before making a choice.

● Practice

1. Look at the pattern below. Which group has the same pattern?

△ ☐ △ ○ △ ☐ △ ○ △ ☐ △ ○

Ⓐ △ ☐ △ ○ △ ☐ △ ○

Ⓑ △ △ △ ☐ ○ △ △ △

Ⓒ ☐ ○ ☐ ○ ☐ ○

2. Look at the pattern in the box. Which item will come next in the pattern?

Ⓕ (cap)

Ⓖ (bat)

Ⓗ (baseball)

GO ON

Name _____ Date_____

● **Lesson 4: Patterns and Place Values (cont.)**

3. **Look at the number pattern in the box. If you count by 2s, what number should be in the blank?**

$$2, \_\_, 6, 8\ 10$$

    Ⓐ 7

    Ⓑ 4

    Ⓒ 12

    Ⓓ 11

4. **Look at the blocks. How many tens are in the picture?**

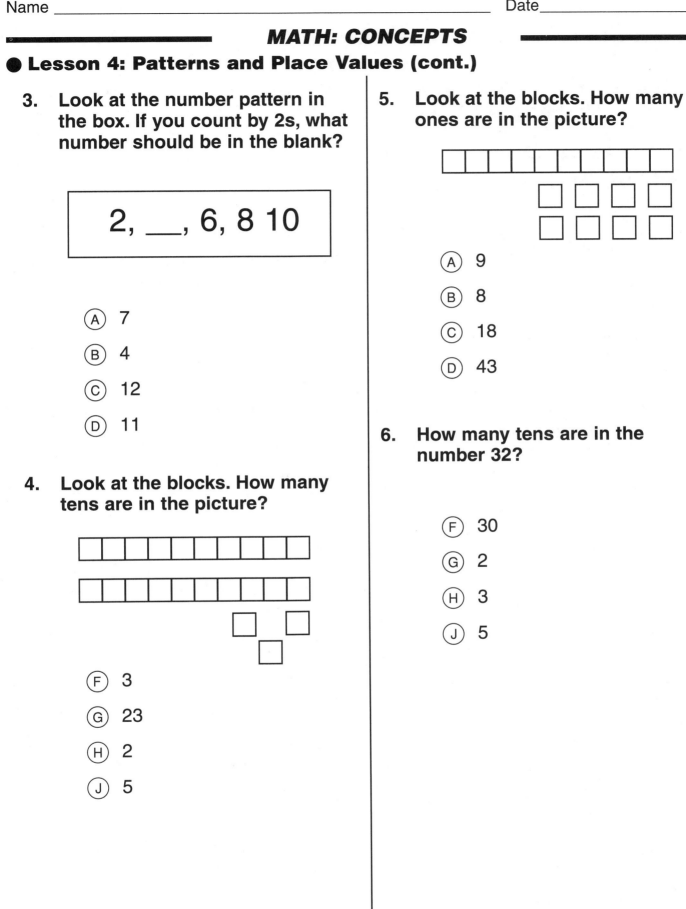

    Ⓕ 3

    Ⓖ 23

    Ⓗ 2

    Ⓙ 5

5. **Look at the blocks. How many ones are in the picture?**

    Ⓐ 9

    Ⓑ 8

    Ⓒ 18

    Ⓓ 43

6. **How many tens are in the number 32?**

    Ⓕ 30

    Ⓖ 2

    Ⓗ 3

    Ⓙ 5

STOP

Name _____   Date_____

MATH: CONCEPTS
SAMPLE TEST

Directions: Look at the pictures. Listen to your teacher read the question. Choose the best answer. Practice with example A.

Example

A.   Which group has the most leaves?

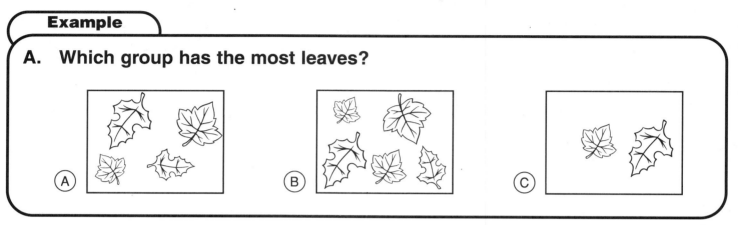

Ⓐ   Ⓑ   Ⓒ

---

1.   Look at the number line. Which number shown is less than 5?

0   5   10   15   20

Ⓐ   0
Ⓑ   5
Ⓒ   20
Ⓓ   15

2.   Count the bubbles. How many bubbles are there all together?

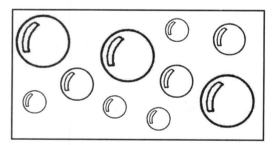

Ⓕ   9
Ⓖ   10
Ⓗ   11
Ⓙ   8

3.   Which numeral is thirty-two?
Ⓐ   302
Ⓑ   5
Ⓒ   132
Ⓓ   32

GO ON

978-1-62057-593-2 *Spectrum Test Practice 1*

MATH: CONCEPTS
SAMPLE TEST (cont.)

4. **Which puppy is second from the bowl?**

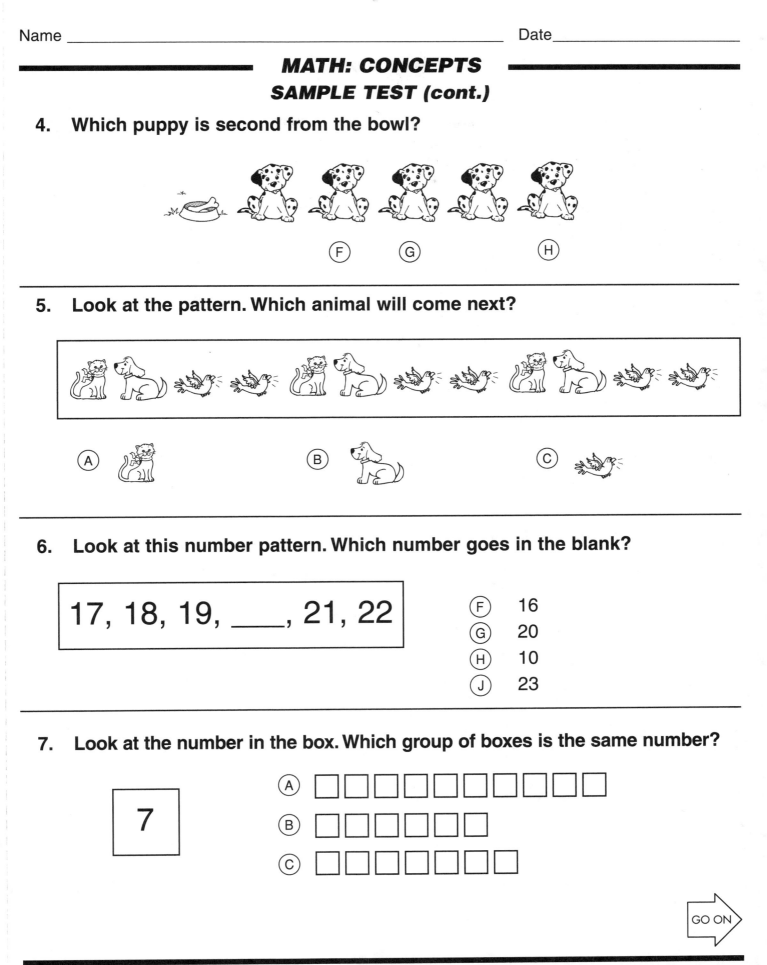

5. **Look at the pattern. Which animal will come next?**

6. **Look at this number pattern. Which number goes in the blank?**

17, 18, 19, ___, 21, 22

F 16
G 20
H 10
J 23

7. **Look at the number in the box. Which group of boxes is the same number?**

7

GO ON

Published by Spectrum. Copyright protected.   978-1-62057-593-2 *Spectrum Test Practice 1*

8. There are 3 flowers. Shelly planted 2 more. Which number sentence tells how many flowers there are?

- (F) 3 − 2 = 1
- (G) 3 + 2 = 5
- (H) 3 + 5 = 8
- (J) 8 − 2 = 6

9. How many tens and ones are there in 31?

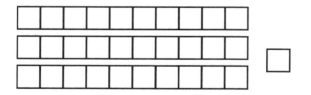

- (A) 3 tens and 1 one
- (B) 30 tens and 1 one
- (C) 1 ten and 30 ones
- (D) 10 tens and 3 ones

10. Look at the blocks. What number do they show?

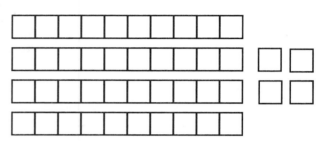

- (F) 404
- (G) 44
- (H) 80
- (J) 14

11. Look at the numbers in the boxes. Which one is in correct counting order?

- (A) | 2, 3, 4, 5 |
- (B) | 13, 14, 16, 17 |
- (C) | 12, 13, 15, 14, |

GO ON

MATH: CONCEPTS
SAMPLE TEST (cont.)

12. Look at the number pattern. Which number is missing?

2, 4, 6, 8, ____

- (F) 1
- (G) 10
- (H) 18
- (J) 9

13. Look at each group. Which does not show 5 items?

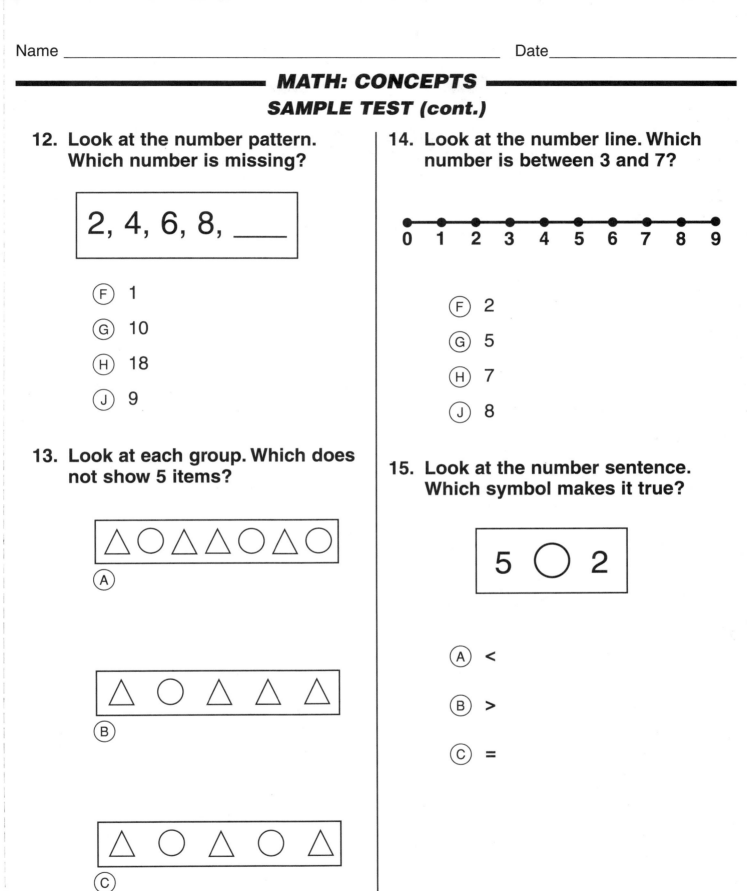

(A)

(B)

(C)

14. Look at the number line. Which number is between 3 and 7?

0 1 2 3 4 5 6 7 8 9

- (F) 2
- (G) 5
- (H) 7
- (J) 8

15. Look at the number sentence. Which symbol makes it true?

5 ◯ 2

- (A) <
- (B) >
- (C) =

STOP

Name _____   Date _____

MATH: COMPUTATION

● Lesson 5: Addition

Directions: Solve each addition problem. Choose "None of these" if the right answer is not given. Practice with examples A and B.

Examples

A.
```
    7
  + 1
```
Ⓐ 9
Ⓑ 8
Ⓒ 6
Ⓓ None of these

B.
```
    1
  + 3
```
Ⓕ 2
Ⓖ 5
Ⓗ 4
Ⓙ None of these

Clue If a problem is too difficult, skip it. Come back to it later if you have time.

● Practice

1.
```
    6
  + 2
```
Ⓐ 5
Ⓑ 11
Ⓒ 8
Ⓓ None of these

3.   5 + 5 = ☐

Ⓐ 5
Ⓑ 55
Ⓒ 10
Ⓓ None of these

2.
```
    2
  + 8
```
Ⓕ 10
Ⓖ 6
Ⓗ 28
Ⓙ None of these

4.   12 + 1 = ☐

Ⓕ 4
Ⓖ 13
Ⓗ 22
Ⓙ None of these

GO ON

978-1-62057-593-2 *Spectrum Test Practice 1*

MATH: COMPUTATION

● Lesson 5: Addition (cont.)

5. $3 + 1 + 4 = \square$

- (A) 8
- (B) 0
- (C) 13
- (D) None of these

6. $6 + 3 + 2 = \square$

- (F) 65
- (G) 11
- (H) 5
- (J) None of these

7.
$$\begin{array}{r} 10 \\ 1 \\ + \ 2 \\ \hline \end{array}$$

- (A) 103
- (B) 7
- (C) 13
- (D) None of these

8. $\square + 11 = 16$

- (F) 5
- (G) 8
- (H) 15
- (J) None of these

9.
$$\begin{array}{r} 3 \\ 8 \\ + \ 5 \\ \hline \end{array}$$

- (A) 16
- (B) 10
- (C) 2
- (D) None of these

10.
$$\begin{array}{r} 13 \\ + \ 5 \\ \hline \end{array}$$

- (F) 8
- (G) 65
- (H) 18
- (J) None of these

STOP

MATH: COMPUTATION

● **Lesson 6: Subtraction**

Directions: Solve each subtraction problem. Choose "None of these" if the right answer is not given. Practice with examples A and B.

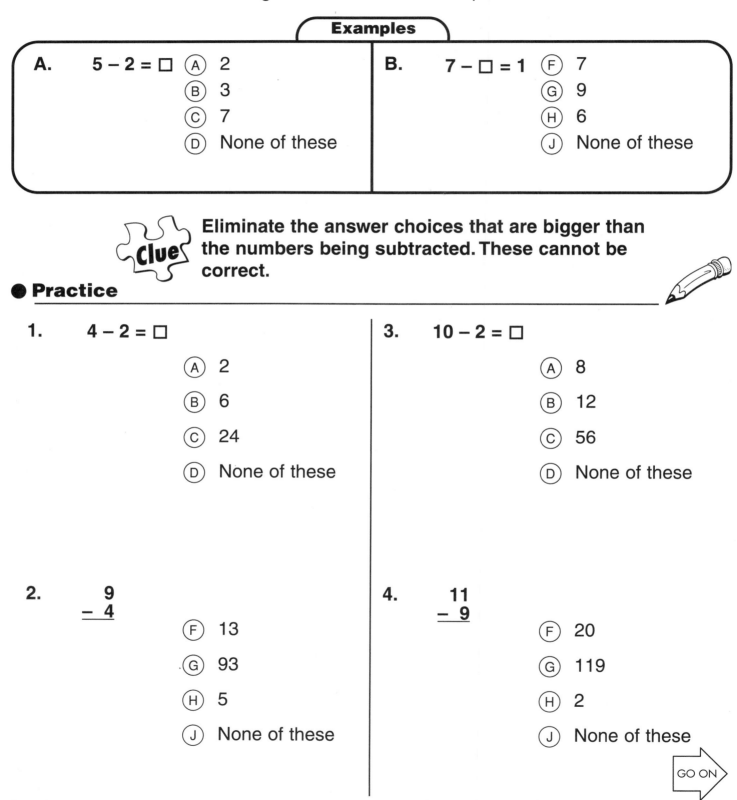

Examples

A. 5 − 2 = ☐
- Ⓐ 2
- Ⓑ 3
- Ⓒ 7
- Ⓓ None of these

B. 7 − ☐ = 1
- Ⓕ 7
- Ⓖ 9
- Ⓗ 6
- Ⓙ None of these

Clue Eliminate the answer choices that are bigger than the numbers being subtracted. These cannot be correct.

● **Practice**

1. 4 − 2 = ☐
- Ⓐ 2
- Ⓑ 6
- Ⓒ 24
- Ⓓ None of these

3. 10 − 2 = ☐
- Ⓐ 8
- Ⓑ 12
- Ⓒ 56
- Ⓓ None of these

2. $\begin{array}{r} 9 \\ -\ 4 \\ \hline \end{array}$
- Ⓕ 13
- Ⓖ 93
- Ⓗ 5
- Ⓙ None of these

4. $\begin{array}{r} 11 \\ -\ 9 \\ \hline \end{array}$
- Ⓕ 20
- Ⓖ 119
- Ⓗ 2
- Ⓙ None of these

GO ON

Name _____   Date_____

MATH: COMPUTATION

● Lesson 6: Subtraction (cont.)

5. $6 - 1 = \square$

(A) 4

(B) 7

(C) 5

(D) None of these

6. $12 - 2 = \square$

(F) 14

(G) 10

(H) 23

(J) None of these

7. $\begin{array}{r} 9 \\ -\ 8 \\ \hline \end{array}$

(A) 17

(B) 98

(C) 89

(D) None of these

8. $9 - 9 = \square$

(F) 99

(G) 0

(H) 18

(J) None of these

9. $\begin{array}{r} 8 \\ -\ 3 \\ \hline \end{array}$

(A) 5

(B) 11

(C) 65

(D) None of these

10. $\begin{array}{r} 3 \\ -\ 2 \\ \hline \end{array}$

(F) 32

(G) 203

(H) 11

(J) None of these

STOP

MATH: COMPUTATION

● **Lesson 7: More Addition and Subtraction**

Directions: Solve each problem. Choose the best answer. Practice with examples A and B.

Examples

A. Which is true?

- (A) $4 + 3 = 10 - 2$
- (B) $5 + 1 = 9 - 4$
- (C) $2 + 4 = 7 - 1$

B. What number is missing?

$5 + \square = 12$

- (F) 6
- (G) 7
- (H) 8

● **Practice**

1. $4 + 9 + 1 = \square$
   - (A) 13
   - (B) 14
   - (C) 15

2. What number is 2 more than 14?
   - (F) 15
   - (G) 16
   - (H) 12

3. What number makes 10 when added to 4?
   - (A) 4
   - (B) 2
   - (C) 6

4. What number is 2 less than 11?
   - (F) 13
   - (G) 10
   - (H) 9

5. Which is equal to $3 + 5 + 5$?
   - (A) $10 + 5$
   - (B) $8 + 3$
   - (C) $10 + 3$

6. Which is true?
   - (F) $12 - 6 = 9 - 3$
   - (G) $8 - 1 = 14 - 8$
   - (H) $15 - 6 = 17 - 9$

GO ON

MATH: COMPUTATION

● **Lesson 7: More Addition and Subtraction (cont.)**

7. Which has the same answer as
$16 - 9 = \square$?

Ⓐ $9 + \square = 16$

Ⓑ $9 + 16 = \square$

Ⓒ $\square - 16 = 9$

8. Which is true?

Ⓕ $5 + 8 = 10 + 3$

Ⓖ $2 + 7 = 5 + 6$

Ⓗ $3 + 1 = 4 + 2$

9. What number is 3 more than 8?

Ⓐ 11

Ⓑ 9

Ⓒ 5

10. $2 + 9 + 8 = \square$

Ⓕ 15

Ⓖ 19

Ⓗ 17

11. Which is equal to $5 + 5 + 5 + 5$?

Ⓐ $5 + 10$

Ⓑ $10 + 10$

Ⓒ 10

12. Which number makes 10 when added to 7?

Ⓕ 3

Ⓖ 13

Ⓗ 7

13. $7 + 6 + 4 = \square$

Ⓐ 11

Ⓑ 13

Ⓒ 17

14. If you know that $12 + 6 = 18$, which do you also know?

Ⓕ $10 + 8 = 18$

Ⓖ $9 + 9 = 18$

Ⓗ $6 + 12 = 18$

STOP

Name _____ Date_____

MATH: COMPUTATION
SAMPLE TEST

Directions: Solve these addition and subtraction problems. Be sure to look closely at the sign. Choose "None of these" if the right answer is not given. Practice with examples A and B. Do numbers 1–12 the same way.

Examples

A. $9 + 1 = \square$
- (A) 10
- (B) 8
- (C) 19
- (D) None of these

B. $\begin{array}{r} 6 \\ -\ 4 \\ \hline \end{array}$
- (F) 5
- (G) 64
- (H) 3
- (J) None of these

---

1. $2 + 5 = \square$
- (A) 3
- (B) 25
- (C) 7
- (D) None of these

4. $\begin{array}{r} 3 \\ +\ 3 \\ \hline \end{array}$
- (F) 6
- (G) 32
- (H) 0
- (J) None of these

2. $11 + 1 = \square$
- (F) 12
- (G) 111
- (H) 115
- (J) None of these

5. $\begin{array}{r} 7 \\ -\ 2 \\ \hline \end{array}$
- (A) 8
- (B) 10
- (C) 5
- (D) None of these

3. $6 - 6 = \square$
- (A) 15
- (B) 109
- (C) 0
- (D) None of these

6. $\begin{array}{r} 13 \\ -\ 0 \\ \hline \end{array}$
- (F) 130
- (G) 4
- (H) 13
- (J) None of these

GO ON →

978-1-62057-593-2 *Spectrum Test Practice 1*

MATH: COMPUTATION
SAMPLE TEST (cont.)

7.   4
      − 1

- (A) 5
- (B) 3
- (C) 123
- (D) None of these

10. $4 + 1 + 0 = \square$

- (F) 415
- (G) 14
- (H) 5
- (J) None of these

8. $8 + 2 = \square$

- (F) 12
- (G) 82
- (H) 16
- (J) None of these

11.   5
      − 4

- (A) 1
- (B) 9
- (C) 20
- (D) None of these

9.   6
      + 4

- (A) 10
- (B) 9
- (C) 42
- (D) None of these

12. $9 + 8 = \square$

- (F) 720
- (G) 980
- (H) 17
- (J) None of these

STOP

MATH: APPLICATIONS

● **Lesson 8: Geometry**

Directions: Listen to your teacher read the problem. Look at the pictures. Choose the best answer for the question. Practice with example A.

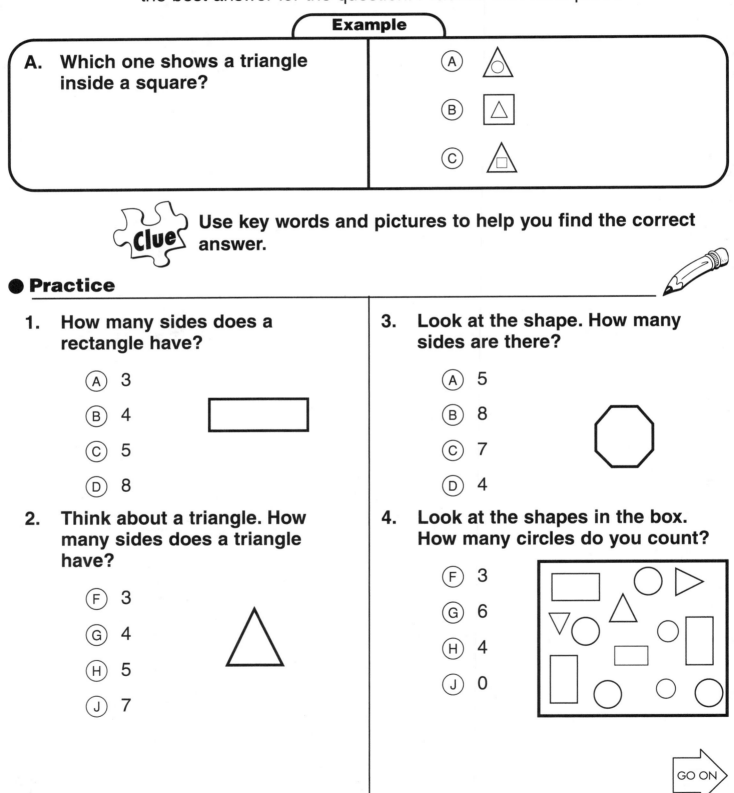

Example

A. Which one shows a triangle inside a square?

Ⓐ
Ⓑ
Ⓒ

Clue Use key words and pictures to help you find the correct answer.

● **Practice**

1. How many sides does a rectangle have?

   Ⓐ 3
   Ⓑ 4
   Ⓒ 5
   Ⓓ 8

2. Think about a triangle. How many sides does a triangle have?

   Ⓕ 3
   Ⓖ 4
   Ⓗ 5
   Ⓙ 7

3. Look at the shape. How many sides are there?

   Ⓐ 5
   Ⓑ 8
   Ⓒ 7
   Ⓓ 4

4. Look at the shapes in the box. How many circles do you count?

   Ⓕ 3
   Ⓖ 6
   Ⓗ 4
   Ⓙ 0

GO ON

MATH: APPLICATIONS

● **Lesson 8: Geometry (cont.)**

5. Look at each group of shapes. Which one has the most stars?

Ⓐ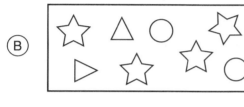

Ⓑ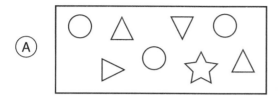

Ⓒ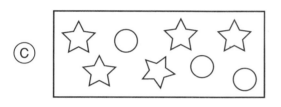

6. Which shape is not a triangle?

Ⓕ

Ⓖ

Ⓗ

7. Look at the shape below. Look at the pictures. Which one is most like the shape below?

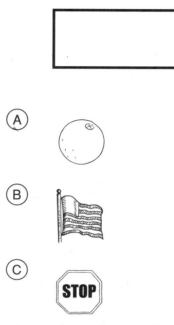

Ⓐ

Ⓑ

Ⓒ

8. Look at the shape. Look at the pictures below. Which one is most like the shape below?

Ⓕ

Ⓖ

Ⓗ

Name _____   Date _____

● **Lesson 9: Geometry**

Directions: Listen to your teacher read the problem. Look at the pictures. Choose the best answer for the question. Practice with example A.

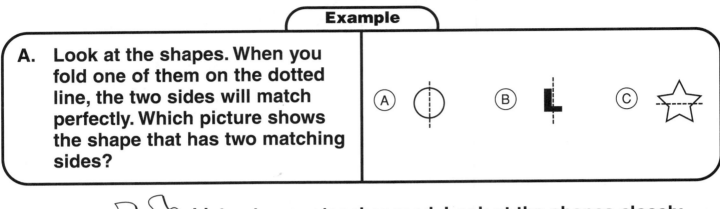

Example

A. Look at the shapes. When you fold one of them on the dotted line, the two sides will match perfectly. Which picture shows the shape that has two matching sides?

Ⓐ   Ⓑ **L**   Ⓒ

Clue Listen to your teacher read. Look at the shapes closely before answering.

● **Practice**

1. Look at the shapes. When you fold one of them on the dotted line, the two sides will match perfectly. Which picture shows the shape that has two matching sides?

Ⓐ
Ⓑ **H**
Ⓒ

2. Look at these shapes. Which one is different?

Ⓕ   Ⓖ   Ⓗ

3. Look at the shapes in the box. How many have four sides?

Ⓐ 2
Ⓑ 4
Ⓒ 5

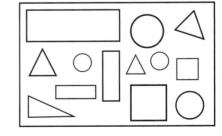

GO ON

MATH: APPLICATIONS

● Lesson 9: Geometry (cont.)

4. **Look at the shapes. Which has the most sides?**

(F)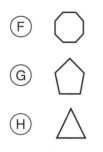

(G)

(H)

5. **Which of these shapes is different from the others?**

(A)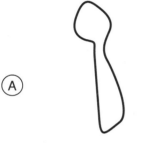

(B)

(C)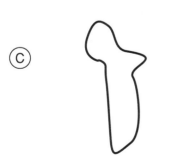

6. **Look at the shape below. Which item below is most like that shape?**

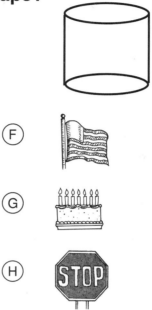

(F)

(G)

(H)

7. **Listen to this riddle. The star is inside the square. The star is not inside the circle. Which picture shows the answer to the riddle?**

(A)

(B)

(C)

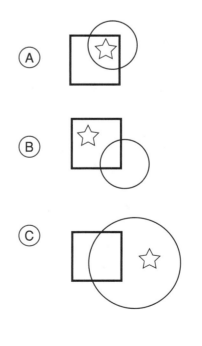

STOP

MATH: APPLICATIONS

● **Lesson 10: Geometry**

Directions: Look at the pictures and solve each problem. Choose the best answer. Practice with example A.

Example

A. **Which part is shaded?**

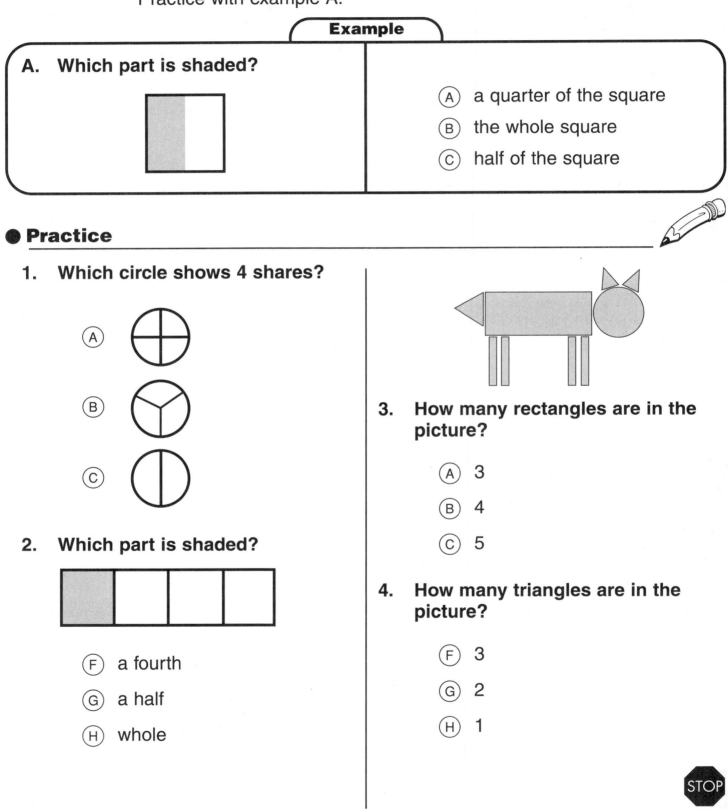

Ⓐ a quarter of the square

Ⓑ the whole square

Ⓒ half of the square

● **Practice**

1. **Which circle shows 4 shares?**

Ⓐ

Ⓑ

Ⓒ

2. **Which part is shaded?**

Ⓕ a fourth

Ⓖ a half

Ⓗ whole

3. **How many rectangles are in the picture?**

Ⓐ 3

Ⓑ 4

Ⓒ 5

4. **How many triangles are in the picture?**

Ⓕ 3

Ⓖ 2

Ⓗ 1

STOP

Name _____ Date_____

MATH: APPLICATIONS

● Lesson 11: Measurement

Directions: Listen to your teacher read the problems. Look at the pictures. Choose the best answer for the question. Practice with example A.

Example

A. Which tool would the doctor use to measure your temperature?

Ⓐ

Ⓑ

Ⓒ

Clue Listen carefully to the problems as you look at the pictures. Then choose the correct answer.

● Practice

1. Look at the fish and cat. Count how many fish long the cat is.

    Ⓐ 4
    Ⓑ 3
    Ⓒ 5

2. Look at the paper clips and pencil. Count how many paper clips long the pencil is.

    Ⓕ 5
    Ⓖ 4
    Ⓗ 3

3. Look at the ruler. About how many inches is the marker?

    Ⓐ 3
    Ⓑ 5
    Ⓒ 6

    1 2 3 4 5 6

    MARKER

GO ON

MATH: APPLICATIONS

● **Lesson 11: Measurement (cont.)**

4. **Look at the ruler. About how many inches is the pair of scissors?**

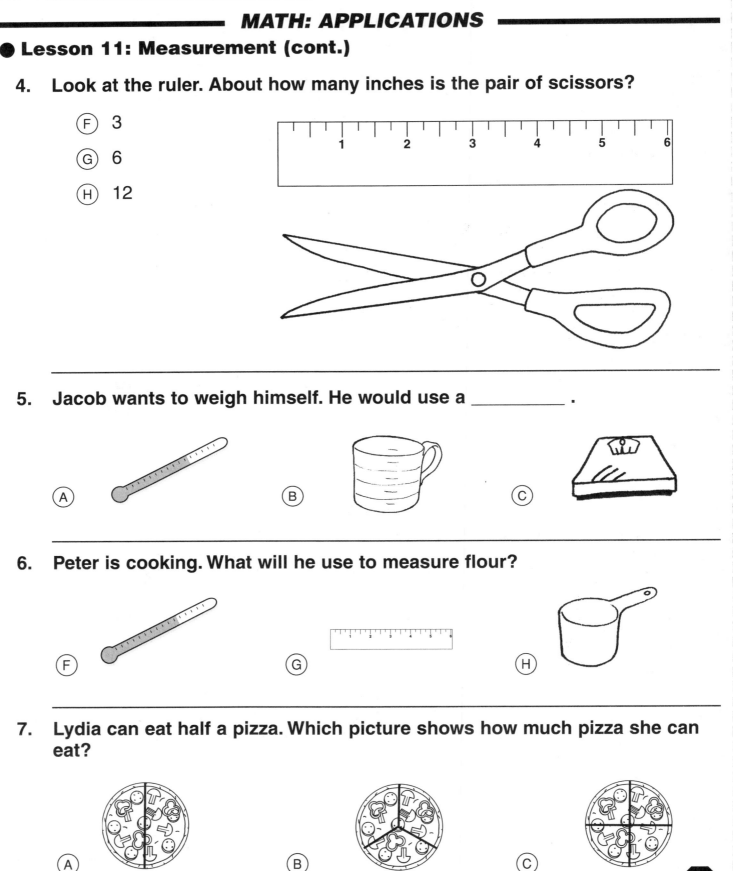

    F 3

    G 6

    H 12

5. **Jacob wants to weigh himself. He would use a _____ .**

    A   B   C

6. **Peter is cooking. What will he use to measure flour?**

    F   G   H

7. **Lydia can eat half a pizza. Which picture shows how much pizza she can eat?**

    A   B   C

STOP

MATH: APPLICATIONS

● **Lesson 12: Measurement**

Directions: Look at the pictures and solve each problem. Choose the best answer. Practice with example A.

Example

A. **Which is longest?**

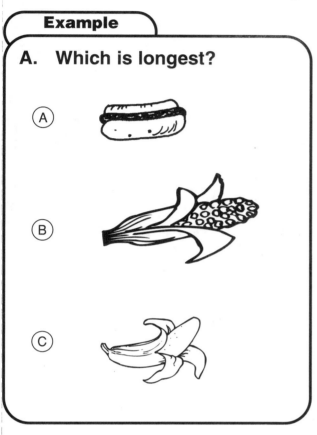

Ⓐ

Ⓑ

Ⓒ

2. **How many paper clips long is the yarn?**

Ⓕ 3

Ⓖ 5

Ⓗ 4

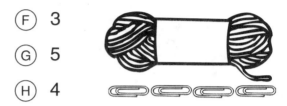

3. **Which shows the puppies in order from shortest to tallest?**

Ⓐ

Ⓑ

Ⓒ

1. **How many blocks long is the carrot?**

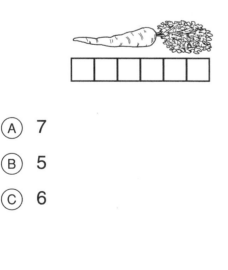

Ⓐ 7

Ⓑ 5

Ⓒ 6

4. **Which lists the alligators in order from longest to shortest?**

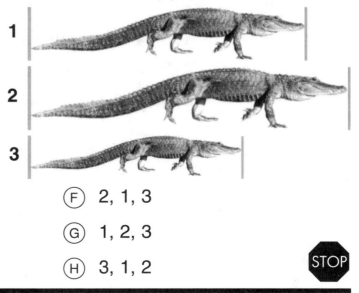

1

2

3

Ⓕ 2, 1, 3

Ⓖ 1, 2, 3

Ⓗ 3, 1, 2

STOP

Name _____ Date_____

● **Lesson 13: Measurement**

Directions: Listen to your teacher read the questions. Look at the pictures. Choose the best answer for each question. Practice with example A.

Example

A. **Which coin is a quarter?**

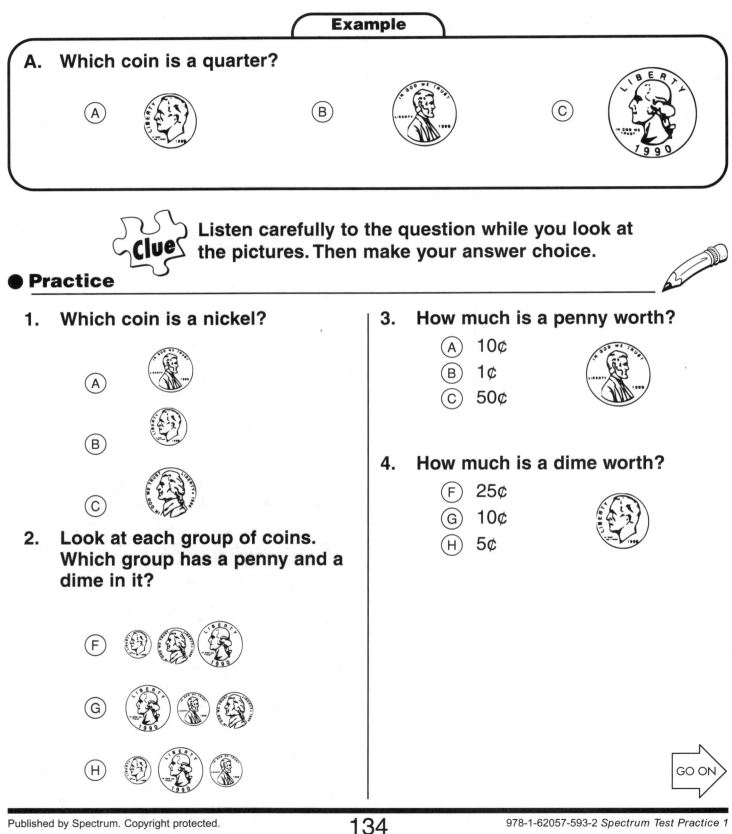

Clue Listen carefully to the question while you look at the pictures. Then make your answer choice.

● **Practice**

1. **Which coin is a nickel?**

Ⓐ

Ⓑ

Ⓒ

2. **Look at each group of coins. Which group has a penny and a dime in it?**

Ⓕ

Ⓖ

Ⓗ

3. **How much is a penny worth?**
   Ⓐ 10¢
   Ⓑ 1¢
   Ⓒ 50¢

4. **How much is a dime worth?**
   Ⓕ 25¢
   Ⓖ 10¢
   Ⓗ 5¢

GO ON →

● **Lesson 13: Measurement (cont.)**

5. Look at the digital clocks. Which one shows the same time as the round clock face?

Ⓐ  1:00

Ⓑ 2:30

Ⓒ 2:00

6. Look at the round clock faces. Which one shows the same time as the digital clock?

 4:30

Ⓕ

Ⓖ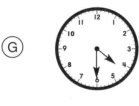

Ⓗ

Look at this page of a calendar. Use it to answer questions 7 and 8.

❀ ❀	MAY				❀ ❀	
SUN	MON	TUE	WED	THU	FRI	SAT
1	2	3	4	5	6	7
8	9	10	11	12	13	14
15	16	17	18	19	20	21
22	23	24	25	26	27	28
29	30	31				

7. What day of the week is May 3?

Ⓐ Tuesday

Ⓑ Wednesday

Ⓒ Friday

8. How many days are in two weeks?

Ⓕ 7

Ⓖ 5

Ⓗ 14

MATH: APPLICATIONS

● **Lesson 14: Problem Solving**

Directions: Listen as your teacher reads the story. Choose the best answer for the question. Practice with example A.

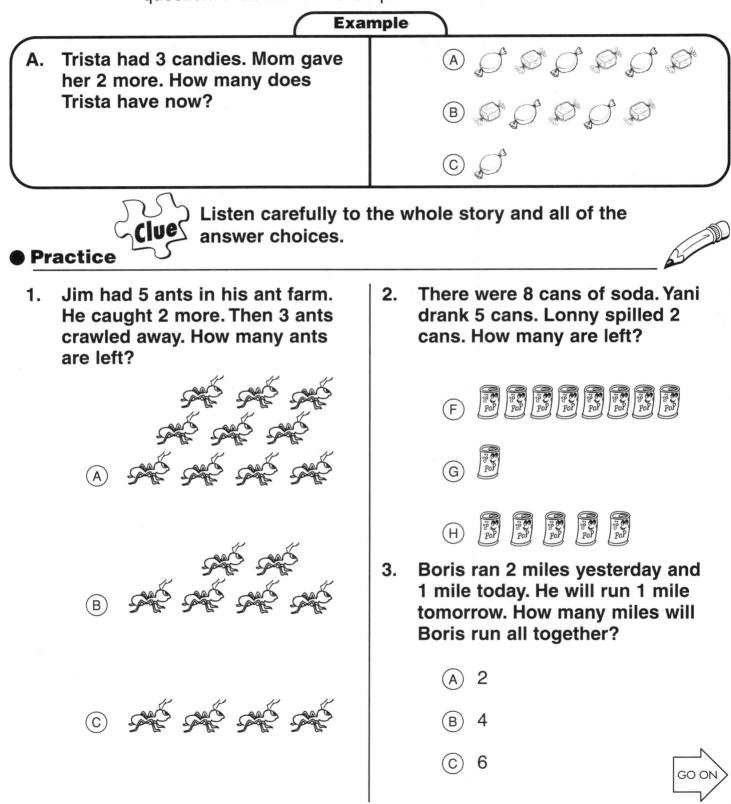

Example

A. Trista had 3 candies. Mom gave her 2 more. How many does Trista have now?

Ⓐ

Ⓑ

Ⓒ

Clue Listen carefully to the whole story and all of the answer choices.

● **Practice**

1. Jim had 5 ants in his ant farm. He caught 2 more. Then 3 ants crawled away. How many ants are left?

Ⓐ

Ⓑ

Ⓒ

2. There were 8 cans of soda. Yani drank 5 cans. Lonny spilled 2 cans. How many are left?

Ⓕ

Ⓖ

Ⓗ

3. Boris ran 2 miles yesterday and 1 mile today. He will run 1 mile tomorrow. How many miles will Boris run all together?

Ⓐ 2

Ⓑ 4

Ⓒ 6

GO ON

Name _____   Date_____

● **Lesson 14: Problem Solving (cont.)**

CLASSROOM PETS

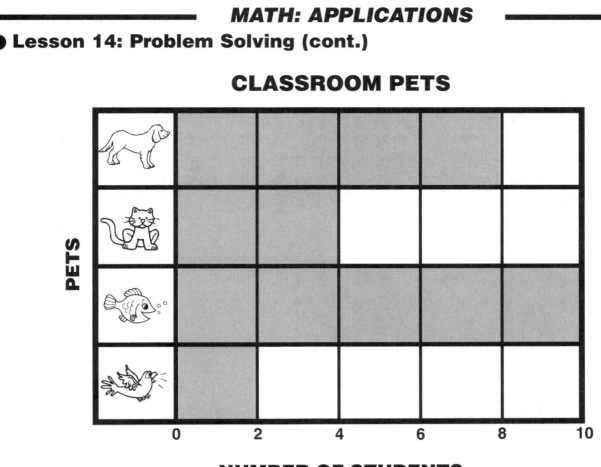

NUMBER OF STUDENTS

Look at the graph. It shows what pets the students have. Use it to answer questions 4–6.

4. **Which pet do 10 students have?**
   - (F) fish
   - (G) dog
   - (H) cat

5. **How many students have cats?**
   - (A) 8
   - (B) 5
   - (C) 4

6. **Which pet is the least popular?**
   - (F) cats
   - (G) fish
   - (H) birds

7. **Ian weighed 45 pounds. He gained one pound last year. He lost 3 pounds this year. How much does Ian weigh now?**
   - (A) 45
   - (B) 43
   - (C) 42

STOP

MATH: APPLICATIONS

● **Lesson 15: Problem Solving**

Directions: Listen to your teacher read the story and the answer choices. Choose the best answer for the question. Practice with examples A and B.

Examples

A. He ate 9 apples. Then he ate 3 more. How many apples did he eat? Which number sentence shows how to find the answer?

(A) $9 + 3 = 12$
(B) $9 - 3 = 6$
(C) $9 - 6 = 3$

B. The plant was 8 inches tall. It was 5 inches when Henry planted it. How much has the plant grown? Which number sentence shows how to find the answer?

(F) $13 - 8 = 5$
(G) $8 + 5 = 13$
(H) $8 - 5 = 3$

Clue Be sure to listen to the whole story. Eliminate the answer choices that you know are wrong.

● **Practice**

1. Jackie's dog had 6 puppies. How many dogs does Jackie have now?

(A) $6 + 0 = 6$
(B) $6 + 1 = 7$
(C) $6 + 2 = 8$

3. Pepe lost 4 stickers this morning. He had 8 stickers last night. How many are left?

(A) $4 + 8 = 12$
(B) $8 - 4 = 4$
(C) $4 - 4 = 0$

2. I go to the movies. It costs $1.00 each time. I went Monday, Tuesday, and Saturday. How much did I spend all together?

(F) $1.00 + $1.00 + $1.00 = $33.00
(G) $1.00 + $1.00 + $1.00 = $3.00
(H) $3.00 + $1.00 = $4.00

4. Mihn ran the race. She won 1 ribbon. If she had 7 ribbons already, how many does she have now?

(F) $7 + 1 = 8$
(G) $7 - 1 = 8$
(H) $1 + 7 = 10$

GO ON

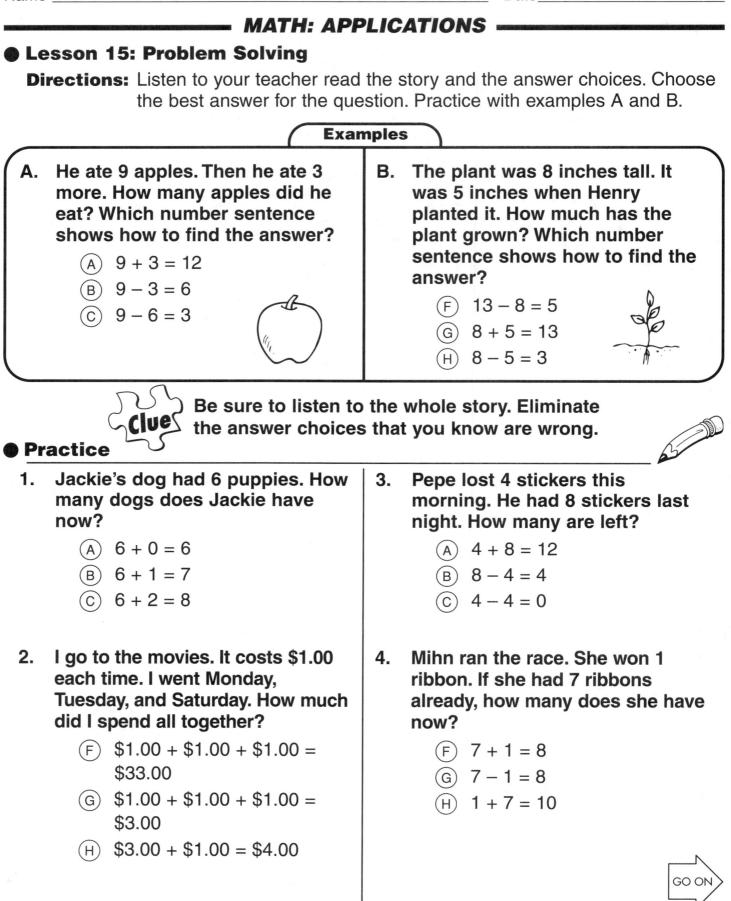

MATH: APPLICATIONS

● **Lesson 15: Problem Solving (cont.)**

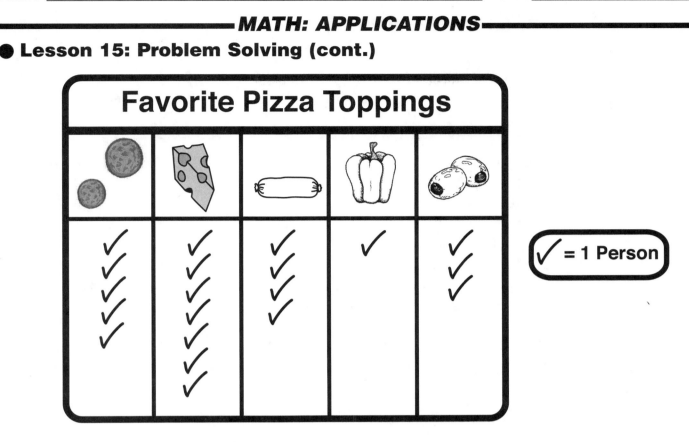

Favorite Pizza Toppings

✓ = 1 Person

Look at the graph. It shows which toppings people like on their pizza. Use it to answer numbers 5–8.

5. **How many people like pepperoni?**
   - (A) 6
   - (B) 5
   - (C) 12

6. **What is the topping most people like?**
   - (F)
   - (G)
   - (H)

7. **How many people all together like cheese and pepperoni?**
   - (A) 12
   - (B) 10
   - (C) 6

8. **What topping is the least favorite?**
   - (F)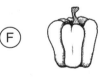
   - (G)
   - (H)

STOP

978-1-62057-593-2 *Spectrum Test Practice 1*

Name _____   Date _____

MATH: APPLICATIONS
SAMPLE TEST

Directions: Listen to your teacher read the problem. Look at the pictures. Choose the best answer for the question. Practice with example A.

Example

A. Look at the shape below. Which of the shapes on the right matches it exactly?

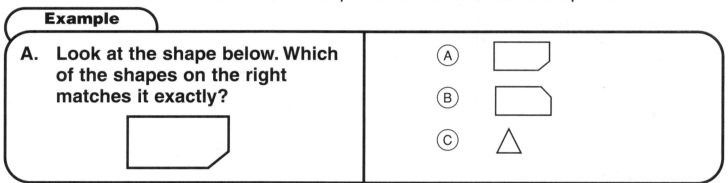

1. Look at the pictures. Which shows a rectangle with a triangle inside?

Ⓐ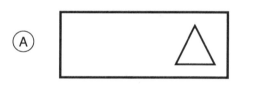

Ⓑ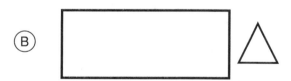

Ⓒ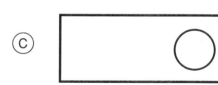

2. Look at these groups of shapes. Which group has 4 circles and 3 stars?

Ⓕ

Ⓖ

Ⓗ

3. How many sides does an octagon have?

Ⓐ 6

Ⓑ 8

Ⓒ 10

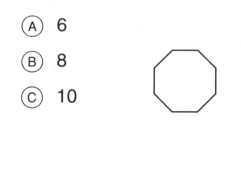

GO ON

MATH: APPLICATIONS
SAMPLE TEST (cont.)

4. Look at the ladder and the paper clips. How many paper clips long is the ladder?

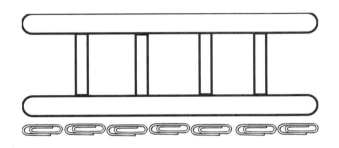

  (F) 6

  (G) 7

  (H) 12

5. Use the ruler. Which animal is the tallest?

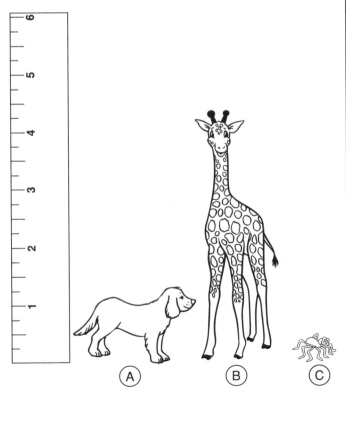

6. Which tool would a mother use to weigh a baby?

  (F)   (G)   (H)

7. Tim, Tom, and Tina split a pie. They ate it all. Each got the same size piece. Which picture shows how they cut the pie?

(A)

(B)

(C)

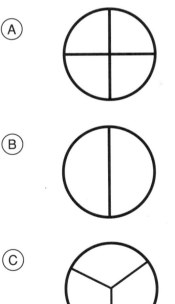

GO ON

8. **Look at the clock face. Find the digital clock that says the same time.**

(F) 11:30

(G) 10:30

(H) 1:00

9. **Look at the digital clock. Find the clock face that says the same time.**

5:15

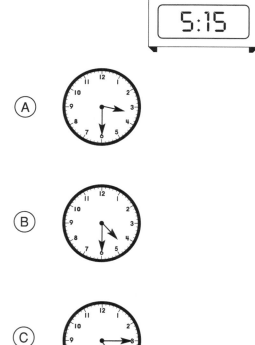

(A)

(B)

(C)

10. **How many days are in one week?**

(F) 5

(G) 7

(H) 10

11. **Justin had 4 coins. He had 13¢ all together. Which group of coins did he have?**

(A)

(B)

(C)

12. **Bart found 1 dime, 1 nickel, and 2 pennies. How much money did Bart find?**

(F) $1.12

(G) 17¢

(H) 12¢

GO ON

Name _____   Date_____

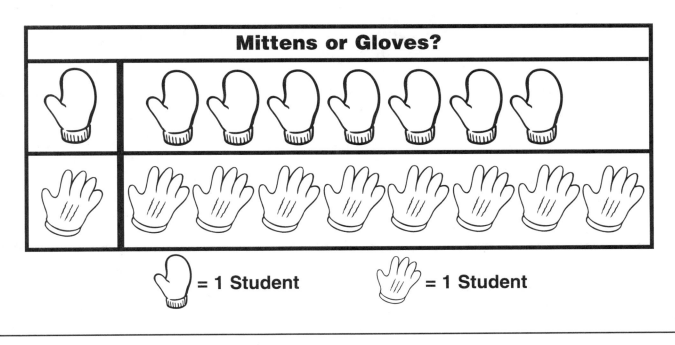

Mittens or Gloves?

 = 1 Student   = 1 Student

---

Look at the graph. It shows how many people like to wear gloves or mittens. Use it to answer questions 13 and 14.

13. How many students like to wear mittens?

   (A) 8

   (B) 7

   (C) 15

14. How many people were asked to tell which they like best?

   (F) 15

   (G) 17

   (H) 8

15. Ned had 10 nails. He found 20 more. How many nails did Ned have?

   (A) $20 - 10 = 10$

   (B) $10 + 20 = 30$

   (C) $10 + 10 = 20$

16. Petra had 9 pennies. She spent 5¢ on a balloon. How much money did she have left?

   (F) $9¢ + 5¢ = 14¢$

   (G) $9¢ - 5¢ = 4¢$

   (H) $5¢ + 9¢ = 32¢$

MATH PRACTICE TEST

● **Part 1: Concepts**

Directions: Listen to your teacher read the question. Look at the pictures. Choose the best answer to the question. Practice together with example A. Do numbers 1–15 the same way.

Example

A. **Count how many stars are in this group.**

(A) 8   (B) 9   (C) 7

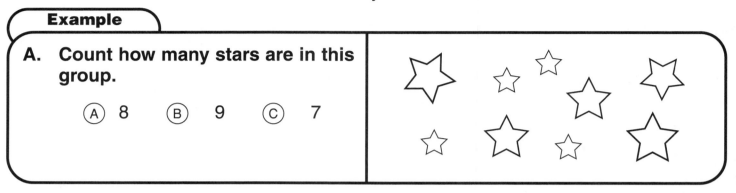

1. **Look at the number in the box. Which group of blocks matches the number?**

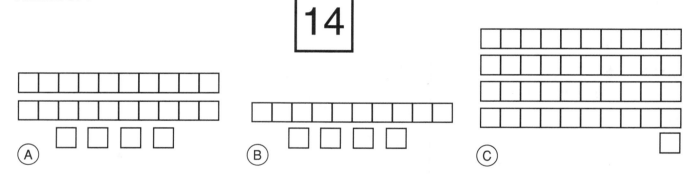

2. **Which vehicle is fourth in line from the left?**

3. **Which plant is the tallest?**

GO ON

978-1-62057-593-2 *Spectrum Test Practice 1*

Name _____   Date_____

4. **Look at the numbers in the box. Put them in order, counting by ones. Which number will be last?**

15, 18, 14, 17, 16

    (F) 14

    (G) 16

    (H) 18

5. **Think about counting by twos. Which number will go in the blank?**

4, 6, ___, 10, 12

    (A) 14

    (B) 8

    (C) 9

6. **Look at the pattern. Which shape should be next?**

    ○ □ □ ☆ ○ □ □ ☆
    ○ □ __

    (F) circle

    (G) star

    (H) square

7. **Look at the pattern. Which number should be next?**

0, 10, 20, ___, 40, 50

    (A) 25

    (B) 32

    (C) 30

GO ON

978-1-62057-593-2 *Spectrum Test Practice 1*

MATH PRACTICE TEST
Part 1: Concepts (cont.)

8. Look at the word in the box. How many letters do you count?

    calendar

    F) 7

    G) 16

    H) 8

9. Which group has the most fish?

    A)

    B)

    C)

10. Count the stars in the boxes. Which group of stars has seven?

    F)

    G)

    H)

11. How many blocks are there in all?

    A) 402

    B) 6

    C) 42

    D) 24

GO ON

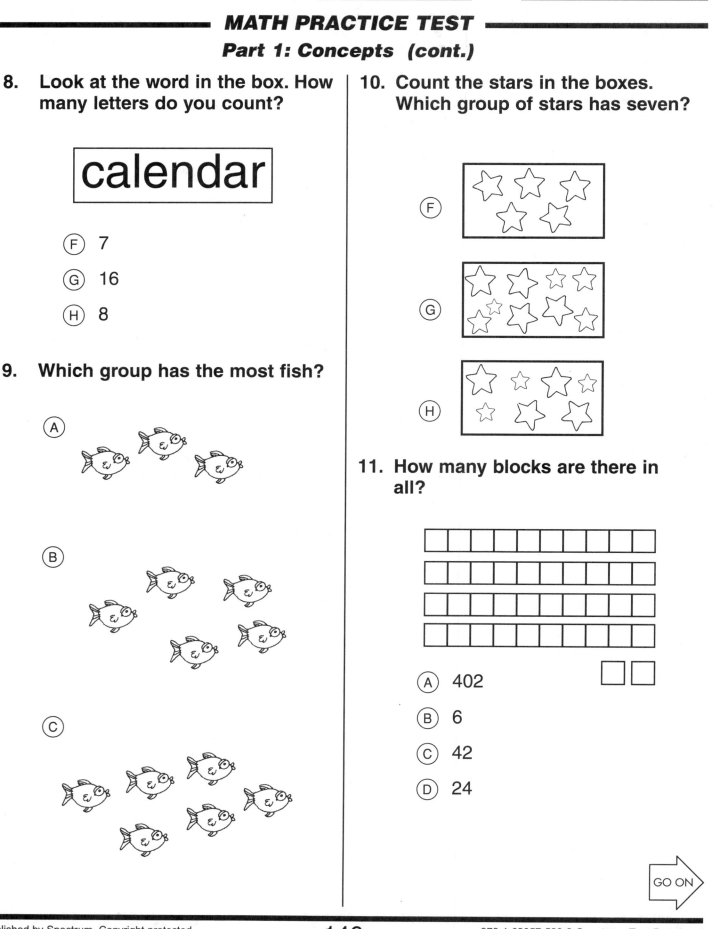

978-1-62057-593-2 *Spectrum Test Practice 1*

MATH PRACTICE TEST
Part 1: Concepts (cont.)

12. How many blocks in all?

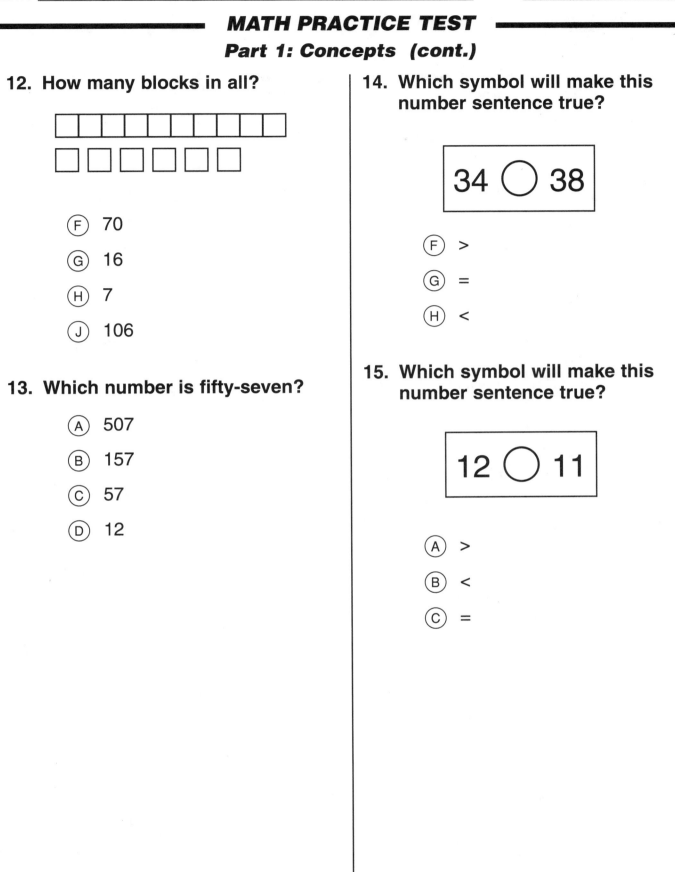

- (F) 70
- (G) 16
- (H) 7
- (J) 106

13. Which number is fifty-seven?

- (A) 507
- (B) 157
- (C) 57
- (D) 12

14. Which symbol will make this number sentence true?

$$34 \bigcirc 38$$

- (F) >
- (G) =
- (H) <

15. Which symbol will make this number sentence true?

$$12 \bigcirc 11$$

- (A) >
- (B) <
- (C) =

STOP

Name _____   Date _____

MATH PRACTICE TEST

● **Part 2: Computation**

Directions: Solve these addition and subtraction problems. Choose the best answer for the question. If none of the answer choices is correct, choose "None of these." Be sure to pay attention to the sign. Practice together with examples A and B. Do the same for 1–18.

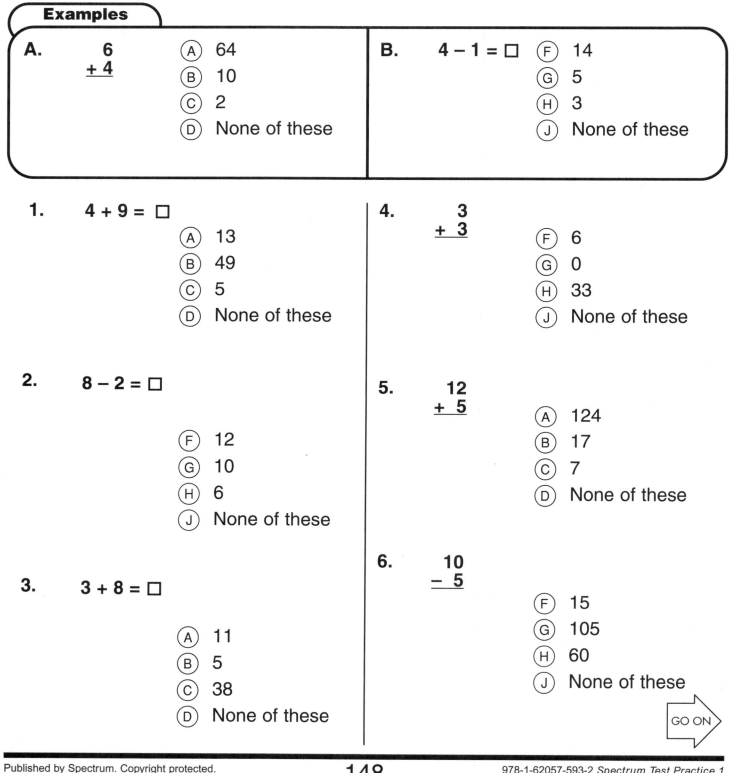

Examples

A.
$$\begin{array}{r} 6 \\ + 4 \\ \hline \end{array}$$
Ⓐ 64
Ⓑ 10
Ⓒ 2
Ⓓ None of these

B. $4 - 1 = \square$
Ⓕ 14
Ⓖ 5
Ⓗ 3
Ⓙ None of these

1. $4 + 9 = \square$
Ⓐ 13
Ⓑ 49
Ⓒ 5
Ⓓ None of these

4.
$$\begin{array}{r} 3 \\ + 3 \\ \hline \end{array}$$
Ⓕ 6
Ⓖ 0
Ⓗ 33
Ⓙ None of these

2. $8 - 2 = \square$
Ⓕ 12
Ⓖ 10
Ⓗ 6
Ⓙ None of these

5.
$$\begin{array}{r} 12 \\ + 5 \\ \hline \end{array}$$
Ⓐ 124
Ⓑ 17
Ⓒ 7
Ⓓ None of these

6.
$$\begin{array}{r} 10 \\ - 5 \\ \hline \end{array}$$
Ⓕ 15
Ⓖ 105
Ⓗ 60
Ⓙ None of these

3. $3 + 8 = \square$
Ⓐ 11
Ⓑ 5
Ⓒ 38
Ⓓ None of these

GO ON ⇨

Name _____ Date _____

7.   7
        − 7

(A) 14

(B) 7

(C) 0

(D) None of these

10.   15 − 2 = □

(F) 13

(G) 17

(H) 132

(J) None of these

8.   25
        + 1

(F) 26

(G) 251

(H) 35

(J) None of these

11.   7
        − 3

(A) 4

(B) 37

(C) 10

(D) None of these

9.   1 + 8 = □

(A) 180

(B) 90

(C) 18

(D) None of these

12.   19
        + 0

(F) 109

(G) 190

(H) 0

(J) None of these

GO ON

MATH PRACTICE TEST
Part 2: Computation (cont.)

13. 1 + 2 + 1 = ☐

(A) 4

(B) 12

(C) 0

(D) None of these

16. 5 + 2 + 2 = ☐

(F) 5

(G) 9

(H) 54

(J) None of these

14. $\begin{array}{r} 9 \\ + 9 \\ \hline \end{array}$

(F) 90

(G) 18

(H) 81

(J) None of these

17. $\begin{array}{r} 17 \\ - 7 \\ \hline \end{array}$

(A) 10

(B) 87

(C) 114

(D) None of these

15. 17 + 2 = ☐

(A) 37

(B) 1,222

(C) 19

(D) None of these

18. 0 + 10 = ☐

(F) 0

(G) 100

(H) 10

(J) None of these

STOP

MATH PRACTICE TEST

● **Part 3: Applications**

Directions: Listen to your teacher read the questions. Look at the answer choices. Choose the best answer for the question. Practice with example A. Do the same for numbers 1–16.

Example

A. Bobbie read 2 books. Howie read 3 books. How many did they read all together?

Ⓐ   Ⓑ   Ⓒ

1. The phone rang 3 times in the morning. It rang 6 times last night. How many times did it ring?

    Ⓐ $3 + 3 = 6$

    Ⓑ $3 + 6 = 9$

    Ⓒ $6 - 3 = 3$

2. I raked 4 bags of leaves. Tyler raked 4 bags. Jess raked 2 bags. How many bags did we end up having?

    Ⓕ $4 + 4 + 2 = 6$

    Ⓖ $4 + 4 + 2 = 10$

    Ⓗ $4 - 4 + 2 = 2$

3. Count each group of coins. Which group is worth the most?

    Ⓐ

    Ⓑ

    Ⓒ

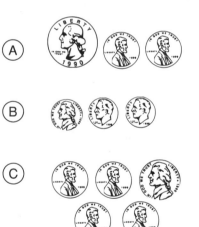

4. Molly had 43¢. She lost 10¢. How much did she have left?

    Ⓕ 7¢

    Ⓖ 33¢

    Ⓗ 42¢

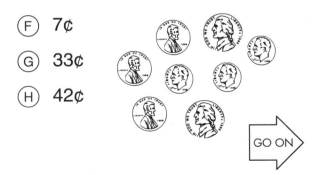

GO ON

978-1-62057-593-2 *Spectrum Test Practice 1*

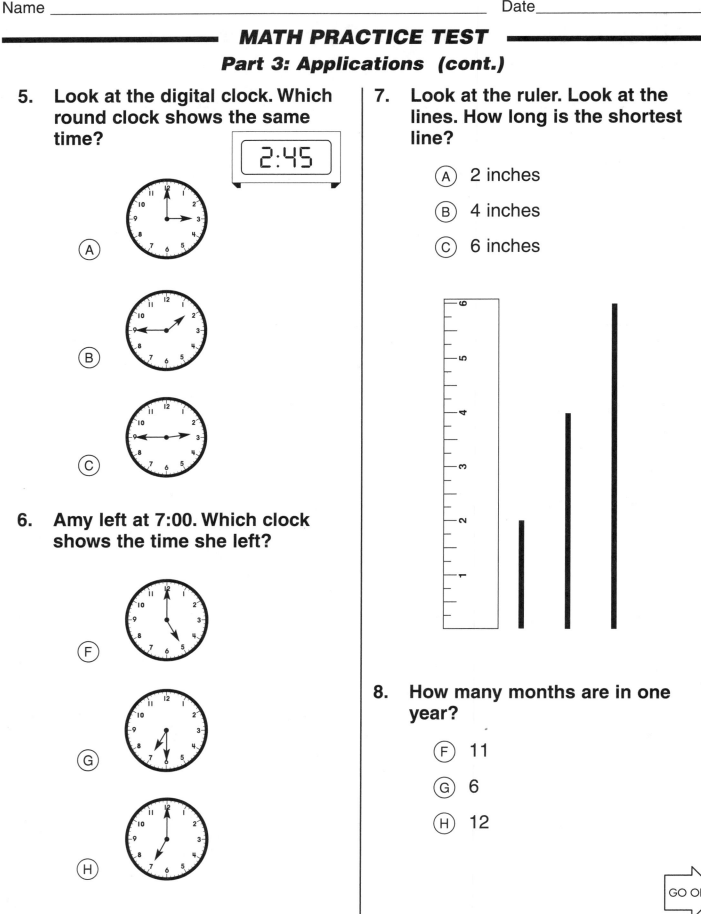

5. **Look at the digital clock. Which round clock shows the same time?**

2:45

(A)

(B)

(C)

6. **Amy left at 7:00. Which clock shows the time she left?**

(F)

(G)

(H)

7. **Look at the ruler. Look at the lines. How long is the shortest line?**

(A) 2 inches

(B) 4 inches

(C) 6 inches

8. **How many months are in one year?**

(F) 11

(G) 6

(H) 12

GO ON

978-1-62057-593-2 Spectrum Test Practice 1

9. How many sides does a rectangle have?

   (A) 3

   (B) 5

   (C) 4

10. Which shape is not the same as the one on the left?

   (F)

   (G)

   (H)

11. Look at the shapes. Which shape can be folded on the dotted line so that the two sides match perfectly?

   (A)

   (B)

   (C)

12. What is the name of this shape?

   (F) circle

   (G) oval

   (H) hexagon

Exercise

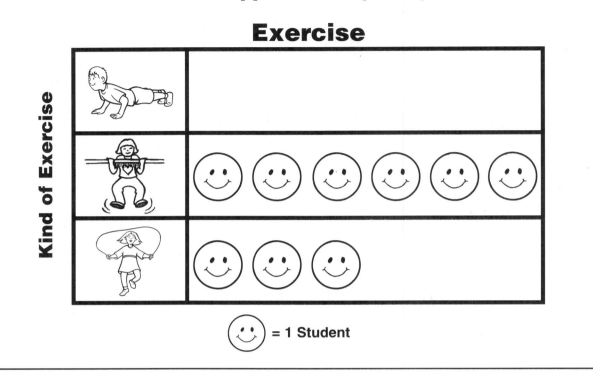

😊 = 1 Student

Look at the chart. It shows which exercises are the most liked by the class. Use it to answer 13–16.

13. How many students liked push-ups?

Ⓐ 0

Ⓑ 5

Ⓒ 3

14. Which exercise was the most liked?

Ⓕ pull-ups

Ⓖ jump rope

Ⓗ push-ups

15. How many students liked either push-ups and pull-ups? Choose the number sentence that solves this problem.

Ⓐ $3 + 6 = 9$

Ⓑ $6 + 0 = 6$

Ⓒ $0 + 5 = 5$

16. How many more students liked pull-ups than jumping rope?

Ⓕ $6 - 5 = 1$

Ⓖ $6 - 3 = 3$

Ⓗ $6 + 5 = 11$

STOP

READING: WORD ANALYSIS
Lesson 1: Letter Recognition
• Page 7
A. C
B. J
1. D
2. F
3. B
4. H

Lesson 2: Beginning Sounds
• Page 8
A. B
1. D
2. F
3. C
4. F

Lesson 3: Ending Sounds
• Page 9
A. B
B. H
1. C
2. F
3. D
4. H
5. B

Lesson 4: Rhyming Words
• Page 10
A. C
1. B
2. H
3. A

Lesson 5: Word Recognition
• Page 11
A. A
B. H
1. C
2. G
3. D
4. G

Lesson 6: Vowel Sounds and Sight Words
• Page 12
A. A
B. F
1. D
2. F
3. B
4. H

Lesson 7: Word Study
• Page 13
A. A
B. G
1. A
2. G
3. A
4. G
5. C

6. G
Sample Test
• Pages 14–16
A. B
1. A
2. G
3. C
4. G
5. C
B. H
C. D
6. F
7. B
8. H
9. B
10. G
11. A
12. G
13. A
14. G
15. C
16. F

READING: VOCABULARY
Lesson 8: Picture Vocabulary
• Page 17
A. B
1. B
2. H
3. C
4. F

Lesson 9: Word Reading
• Page 18
A. C
B. F
1. A
2. F
3. B
4. H
5. C
6. G

Lesson 10: Word Meaning
• Page 19
A. B
B. F
1. C
2. G
3. C
4. F
5. A
6. H

Lesson 11: Word Parts
• Page 20
A. B
1. A
2. H
3. A

B. F
4. F
5. B
6. G

Lesson 12: Word Relationships
• Page 21
A. B
B. F
1. C
2. H
3. A
4. F
5. C
6. H

Lesson 13: Synonyms
• Page 22
A. A
B. G
1. C
2. F
3. C
4. J
5. C
6. H

Lesson 14: Antonyms
• Page 23
A. C
B. J
1. B
2. F
3. C
4. F
5. D
6. H

Lesson 15: Words in Context
• Page 24
A. C
B. G
1. B
2. H
3. D
4. F

Sample Test
• Pages 25–28
A. B
1. C
2. F
3. A
4. F
B. F
C. C
5. B
6. H
7. A
8. G
9. C
10. F

11. B
12. F
13. C
14. F
15. C
16. J
17. B
18. F
19. C
20. F
21. C
22. J

READING: READING COMPREHENSION

Lesson 16: Listening Comprehension
• Page 29

A. B
1. C
2. H
3. C

Lesson 17: Picture Comprehension
• Page 30

A. A
1. B
2. F
3. B
4. H

Lesson 18: Sentence Comprehension
• Page 31

A. A
B. G
1. A
2. H
3. B
4. H

Lesson 19: Fiction
• Page 32

A. B
1. B
2. F

Lesson 20: Fiction
• Page 33

1. B
2. F
3. C
4. G

Lesson 21: Reading Literature
• Pages 34–35

1. A
2. H
3. B
4. F
5. B

6. F
7. C
8. G
9. A
10. H

Lesson 22: Nonfiction
• Page 36

1. B
2. F
3. C
4. F

Lesson 23: Nonfiction
• Page 37

1. A
2. H
3. B
4. G

Sample Test
• Pages 38–40

A. B
1. A
2. H
3. B
4. G
5. A
6. H
7. A
8. H
9. B
10. F
11. C

READING PRACTICE TEST
• Pages 41–55
Part 1: Word Analysis

A. D
1. D
2. F
3. B
4. H
5. A
B. F
C. C
6. G
7. A
8. H
9. B
D. H
10. G
11. A
12. G
13. A
14. F
15. B
E. A
F. F
16. G

17. A
18. F
19. B

Part 2: Vocabulary

A. B
1. C
2. F
3. B
4. F
B. F
C. B
5. C
6. F
7. A
8. G
9. B
10. F
11. A
12. F
D. B
13. A
14. H
15. D
16. H
17. B
18. F
19. B
20. G
21. A
22. H

Part 3: Reading Comprehension

A. C
1. C
2. H
B. F
3. C
4. G
5. A
6. G
C. B
7. C
8. F
9. A
10. F
D. G
11. B
12. G
13. A
14. G
15. B
16. F
17. A
18. G
19. B
20. F
21. C
22. G

23. A
24. G
25. B
26. F

LANGUAGE: LISTENING
Lesson 1: Listening Skills
• Pages 56–57
A. A
1. B
2. H
3. C
4. H
5. A
6. H
Lesson 2: Listening Skills
• Page 58
A. A
B. G
1. C
2. G
3. A
4. G
5. B
Lesson 3: Language Skills
• Pages 59–60
A. B
1. A
2. G
3. A
4. F
5. C
6. H
7. B
Sample Test
• Pages 61–63
A. C
1. A
2. H
3. B
4. F
5. A
6. F
B. F
C. B
7. B
8. F
9. B
10. H

LANGUAGE: LANGUAGE MECHANICS
Lesson 4: Capitalization
• Page 64
A. C
B. F
1. D

2. H
3. A
4. H
Lesson 5: Capitalization
• Page 65
A. B
1. A
2. G
B. H
3. C
4. F
5. C
Lesson 6: Punctuation
• Page 66
A. B
B. H
1. A
2. G
3. B
4. F
5. B
6. F
Lesson 7: Punctuation
• Page 67
A. B
1. C
2. G
B. G
3. C
4. F
Lesson 8: Capitalization and Punctuation
• Page 68
A. A
B. H
1. C
2. G
3. C
4. H
5. A
6. G
Sample Test
• Pages 69–73
A. D
1. B
2. F
3. D
4. F
5. A
6. J
B. F
C. B
7. B
8. F
9. C
10. F
D. G

11. B
12. G
13. B
14. G
15. B
16. G
E. B
17. A
18. F
19. A
20. G
F. G
21. B
22. F
23. B
24. F
25. B
26. G

LANGUAGE: LANGUAGE EXPRESSION
Lesson 9: Usage
• Page 74
A. C
B. H
1. B
2. F
3. C
4. H
5. C
6. G
Lesson 10: Usage
• Page 75
A. C
B. H
1. B
2. G
3. C
4. F
5. C
6. G
Lesson 11: Adjectives and Conjunctions
• Page 76
A. B
B. F
1. C
2. G
3. B
4. G
5. C
6. H
Lesson 12: Determiners and Prepositions
• Page 77
A. B
B. H

1. C
2. F
3. A
4. F
5. A
6. G

Lesson 13: Pronouns
• Page 78
A. C
B. F
1. B
2. G
3. A
4. H
5. B
6. H

Lesson 14: Sentences
• Page 79
A. B
B. G
1. C
2. F
3. B
4. F

Lesson 15: Sentences
• Page 80
A. B
B. H
1. B
2. F
3. C
4. H
5. C
6. F

Lesson 16: Paragraphs
• Page 81
A. B
1. A
2. G
3. B
4. G

Sample Test
• Pages 82–84
A. A
1. A
2. G
3. C
B. H
4. H
5. B
6. G
C. B
7. C
8. F
9. C
D. G
10. F

11. B
12. H
E. A
13. C
14. G
15. A
F. F
16. G
17. C
18. F

LANGUAGE: SPELLING
Lesson 17: Spelling Skills
• Page 85
A. A
B. G
1. C
2. G
3. A
4. G
5. B
6. H

Lesson 18: Spelling Skills
• Page 86
A. C
B. F
1. B
2. F
3. C
4. G
5. B
6. F

Sample Test
• Pages 87–88
A. B
B. F
1. C
2. F
3. B
4. H
5. A
6. F
C. A
D. H
7. A
8. H
9. B
10. H
11. C
12. F

LANGUAGE: STUDY SKILLS
Lesson 19: Study Skills
• Page 89
A. B
1. A
2. H

3. A
B. G
4. F
5. B

Lesson 20: Study Skills
• Page 90
A. C
1. A
2. G
3. C

Sample Test
• Page 91
A. C
B. F
1. C
2. F
3. C
4. F
5. B

LANGUAGE PRACTICE TEST
• Pages 94–105
Part 1: Listening
A. C
1. B
2. F
3. C
4. H
5. B
6. F
7. C
B. F
8. G
9. C
10. F

Part 2: Language Mechanics
A. A
B. G
1. A
2. G
3. A
4. F
C. B
5. A
6. G
7. A
8. H
D. G
E. B
9. B
10. G
11. B
12. G
13. A
14. F
F. G
G. A

15. C
16. F
17. C
18. H
19. C
20. F

Part 3: Language Expression
A. C
1. B
2. G
3. C
B. H
4. G
5. C
6. F
C. B
7. B
8. F
9. A
D. F
10. F
11. B

Part 4: Spelling
A. A
B. H
1. C
2. F
3. C
4. G
5. C
6. F
C. C
D. G
7. C
8. F
9. C
10. G
11. B
12. H

Part 5: Study Skills
A. A
1. B
2. G
3. B
4. H

MATH: CONCEPTS
Lesson 1: Numeration
• Pages 106–107
A. C
1. C
2. G
3. A
4. J
5. B
6. G
7. B

Lesson 2: Sequencing
• Pages 108–109
A. A
1. C
2. H
3. B
4. G
5. A
6. G
7. A

Lesson 3: Number Concepts
• Pages 110–111
A. B
1. B
2. G
3. C
4. H
5. C
6. G
7. B

Lesson 4: Patterns and Place Values
• Pages 112–113
A. B
1. A
2. G
3. B
4. H
5. B
6. H

Sample Test
• Pages 114–117
A. B
1. A
2. G
3. D
4. F
5. A
6. G
7. C
8. G
9. A
10. G
11. A
12. G
13. A
14. G
15. B

MATH: COMPUTATION
Lesson 5: Addition
• Pages 118–119
A. B
B. H
1. C
2. F
3. C

4. G
5. A
6. G
7. C
8. F
9. A
10. H

Lesson 6: Subtraction
• Pages 120–121
A. B
B. H
1. A
2. H
3. A
4. H
5. C
6. G
7. D
8. G
9. A
10. J

Lesson 7: More Addition and Subtraction
• Pages 122–123
A. C
B. G
1. B
2. G
3. C
4. H
5. C
6. F
7. A
8. F
9. A
10. G
11. B
12. F
13. C
14. H

Sample Test
• Pages 124–125
A. A
B. J
1. C
2. F
3. C
4. F
5. C
6. H
7. B
8. J
9. A
10. H
11. A
12. H

MATH: APPLICATIONS
Lesson 8: Geometry
• Pages 126–127
- A. B
- 1. B
- 2. F
- 3. B
- 4. G
- 5. C
- 6. F
- 7. B
- 8. F

Lesson 9: Geometry
• Pages 128–129
- A. A
- 1. B
- 2. H
- 3. C
- 4. F
- 5. C
- 6. G
- 7. B

Lesson 10: Geometry
• Page 130
- A. C
- 1. A
- 2. F
- 3. C
- 4. F

Lesson 11: Measurement
• Pages 131–132
- A. C
- 1. B
- 2. F
- 3. B
- 4. G
- 5. C
- 6. H
- 7. A

Lesson 12: Measurement
• Page 133
- A. B
- 1. C
- 2. H
- 3. A
- 4. F

Lesson 13: Measurement
• Pages 134–135
- A. C
- 1. C
- 2. H
- 3. B
- 4. G
- 5. C
- 6. G
- 7. A
- 8. H

Lesson 14: Problem Solving
• Pages 136–137
- A. B
- 1. C
- 2. G
- 3. B
- 4. F
- 5. C
- 6. H
- 7. B

Lesson 15: Problem Solving
• Pages 138–139
- A. A
- B. H
- 1. B
- 2. G
- 3. B
- 4. F
- 5. B
- 6. G
- 7. A
- 8. F

Sample Test
• Pages 140–143
- A. A
- 1. A
- 2. H
- 3. B
- 4. G
- 5. B
- 6. G
- 7. C
- 8. G
- 9. C
- 10. G
- 11. C
- 12. G
- 13. B
- 14. F
- 15. B
- 16. G

MATH PRACTICE TEST
• Pages 144–154
Part 1: Concepts
- A. B
- 1. B
- 2. F
- 3. C
- 4. H
- 5. B
- 6. H
- 7. C
- 8. H
- 9. C
- 10. H
- 11. C
- 12. G
- 13. C
- 14. H
- 15. A

Part 2: Computation
- A. B
- B. H
- 1. A
- 2. H
- 3. A
- 4. F
- 5. B
- 6. J
- 7. C
- 8. F
- 9. D
- 10. F
- 11. A
- 12. J
- 13. A
- 14. G
- 15. C
- 16. G
- 17. A
- 18. H

Part 3: Applications
- A. B
- 1. B
- 2. G
- 3. A
- 4. G
- 5. C
- 6. H
- 7. A
- 8. H
- 9. C
- 10. H
- 11. A
- 12. G
- 13. A
- 14. F
- 15. B
- 16. G